To Coach Andy Talley -

Thank you for speaking at the 2019 Army West Point Coaches Clinic. It's an honor to have you join our team.

Congratulations on a tremendous career and all that you have done for college football.

BEAT navy!

Jeff Monken

WEST POINT
AN INSIDE LOOK AT
THE LONG GRAY LINE

WRITING BY
LINDA FOSTER

FOREWORD BY
GENERAL H. NORMAN SCHWARZKOPF

PHOTOGRAPHY BY
ROGER MILLER

CADETS LINE UP BEFORE REVIEW

ROGER CHARLES MILLER IN HIS BALTIMORE STUDIO

image publishing, ltd.
1411 Hollins Street / Union Square
Baltimore, MD 21223-2417

TEL 410.566.1222   FAX 410.233.1241
WEB PAGE roger**miller**photo.com

DEDICATION

I would like to dedicate this book to our troops who are serving our country around the world, particularly in Iraq and Afghanistan. We pray for the safe return of our relatives, friends, and countrymen.

ROGER MILLER 06-30-2007

SPECIAL ACKNOWLEDGMENTS

Sincere thanks to **GEN H. NORMAN SCHWARZKOPF**, (Ret.) for writing the foreword to this book and allowing me to meet and photograph him at Trophy Point.

Sincere thanks to **GEN BARRY McCAFFREY**, (Ret.) for writing his part of the Notable Graduates chapter and allowing me to photograph him at his Washington office.

Sincere thanks to **ASTRONAUT BUZZ ALDRIN**, (Ret.) for writing his part of the Notable Graduates chapter and for allowing me to meet him in New York and take his photograph.

Sincere thanks to **GEN WAYNE A. DOWNING**, (Ret.) for writing his part of the Notable Graduates chapter and allowing me to meet and photograph him at Lincoln Hall.

Sincere thanks to **BG REBECCA STEVENS HALSTEAD** for writing her part of the Notable Graduates chapter and allowing me to meet and photograph her at Aberdeen Proving Grounds.

Sincere thanks to **LTC WILLIAM ADAMS**, (Ret.) for his important help with creating this book and his love of West Point.

Sincere thanks to **MICHAEL D'AQUINO** our PAO host, and expert, and **THERESA BRINKERHOFF** our PAO project officer, and guide.

Sincere thanks to **DR. MIKE MATTHEWS** professor in Behavioral Sciences and Leadership for his help and assistance with this book and his love of West Point.

Sincere thanks to **JAROMIR STEPHANY** my instructor in photography, mentor and friend since college. Sincere thanks to **JACK RAE** who has forgotten more about my Nikon than I ever knew. Sincere thanks to **TOM BECK** Curator of Photography at UMBC for being able to put words to what I do in my photography and reminding me I have a long way to go.

ROGER MILLER and LINDA FOSTER 06-30-2007

INFORMATION - COPYRIGHT

GENERAL ACKNOWLEDGMENTS

We would like to thank the following: **LTG FRANKLIN L. HAGENBACK, SUPERINTENDENT** for allowing us to photograph and understand West Point; **LTG WILLIAM JAMES LENOX,** (Ret.) **previous SUPERINTENDENT** whom we began this book with, and his wife for allowing us to photograph Quarters 100; **BG ROBERT L. CASLEN, COMMANDANT OF CADETS,** for allowing us to photograph his cadets and his assistance with the book; **BG PATRICK FINNEGAN, DEAN** for his help with the book; **LTC KENT CASSELLA** for his assistance with the book; **COL JOHN CALABRO,** (Ret.) of the Association of Graduates for his help with the Notable Graduates; **MAJ MICHAEL RITTENHOUSE** for his assistance with photographing the uniforms, cadet rooms and TAC officer and enlisted - a safe return from Kuwait; **BOB BERETTA** for getting us press credentials for the Army-Navy game; **MAJ MICHAEL TITUS** for his help and assistance and insight with military instruction; **MAJ CHRISTOPHER McKINNEY** for his brilliant assessment of cordon and search at Camp Buckner during Media Day; **MAJ WES YOUNG** for his assistance with Calvary training at Ft. Knox, we are so glad we did not miss you; **MAJ MATT DeLOIA** for being our guide and mentor at Ft. Knox; **MAJ BRIAN DIETZMAN** for his guidance through summer training at Camp Buckner; **MAJ JERRY PATAK** for his help with setting up our schedule for summer training; **MAJ TONY JONES** and **MAJ FRANK LEIJA** for their assistance with Air Assault at both Camp Buckner and Camp Smith; **SFC MIKE RICKLEFS** for allowing me to fly with the Black Knights and get some great photographs of the team and the campus; **SFC SHANE CARROLL** for his help with the photographs of Quarters 100; to all the **CADETS** that helped us photograph the uniforms especially **CADET VINKO WHITE** who got the "privilege" of setting things up and carrying his weapon all afternoon for the photographs; to all the **CADETS AT WEST POINT** who allowed us to be a part of their lives, photograph their experiences and who were informative, gracious hosts, one and all; to all the **FACULTY OF WEST POINT** who allowed us to photograph and be a part of their instruction and helped us understand what was happening. Their assistance and enthusiasm reflects their dedication to the cadets, West Point and our Country. We would particularly like to thank the following: **MAJ ERIC BULLER, COL DAISIE BOETTNER, LTC KARL MEYER, COL DAVE BEDEY, LTC WILLIE McFADDEN, COL GENE PALKA, LTC SHELLEY ECONOM, COL KIP NYGREN, and COL PATRICK SWEENEY.**

ROGER MILLER, and LINDA FOSTER 06-30-2007

PUBLISHER'S DISCLAIMER

CREDITS

Photography by **ROGER CHARLES MILLER**
Design and Layout by **ROGER CHARLES MILLER**
Foreword by **GENERAL H. NORMAN SCHWARZKOPF**
Writing by **LINDA MARSHA FOSTER**
Editing by **ROGER MILLER AND LINDA FOSTER**
Photograph Page 5 by **C. RUSSELL, ACADEMY PHOTO, WEST POINT, N.Y.**

Printed in China.

ORDERS

For direct orders please call or write for the specific pricing and the postage and handling to **IMAGE PUBLISHING, LTD.** at the above address. Discounts are available for stores, institutions and corporations, with minimum order requirements. You may also contact us for sales through our web page. The suggested retail price at the time of publication is **US$44.50.**

This detail on the large stained glass window at the front of the Cadet Chapel is a summary of the ideals of West Point, **"DUTY, HONOR, COUNTRY"** The sanctuary window was the first installed and was built "To the Glory of the God of Battles and the Faithful Memory of the Departed Graduates of the United States Military Academy." All the windows in the Chapel were removed, cleaned and releaded from 1998 to 1999 so that their beauty could be perserved for future cadets to appreciate.

3

It's been said that **EVERYONE LOVES A PARADE.** During graduation week, there is a parade, review or rehearsal everyday and it is a credit to cadets that they look so sharp: The sun is hot and cadets are in Full Dress Uniform complete with a black dress hat sometimes called the "tar-bucket." Most people would find it difficult to look crisp and cool but cadets pull it off well.

CONTENTS

GENERAL H. NORMAN SCHWARZKOPF graduated from West Point in 1956. During his 35 years of service, he commanded Army units from platoon through army field level. He served two combat tours in the Republic of Vietnam, served as the Deputy Commander of the Joint Task Force in charge of U.S. Forces participating in the Grenada student rescue operation, and served as the Commander of U.S. and Allied Forces during Operations Desert Shield/Desert Storm. He authored the best-selling book, *It Doesn't Take a Hero*, is an avid champion of charities benefitting sick children and a staunch advocate of cancer research. General Schwarzkopf lives his life exemplifying the West Point credo "Duty, Honor, Country," and continually validates his profound love of humanity and our country.

FOREWORD
BY GENERAL H. NORMAN SCHWARZKOPF

From the time I was a young boy, I knew I was destined to attend West Point. I was raised in New Jersey with my two older sisters. We lived in a house that dated back to the War of 1812 and is now part of a school. My father, ultimately a two-star Army General, graduated from West Point and fought in World War II. At an early age, he instilled in me the West Point credo of "Duty, Honor, Country." When he was assigned to Iran for an extended period, he presented me with his West Point sword and charged me with the duty of caring for the family. That was quite a responsibility and honor for a 10-year old boy. At the end of World War II, my father continued to serve in Iran, and I had the opportunity to join him and attend school in Iran for over a year. My parents wanted to be sure I received a good education, so they sent me to school in Switzerland for my high school years. My exposure to the culture in Iran, Switzerland and other countries, taught me firsthand how to work with people of different backgrounds. Throughout my entire career, particularly in the latter years in the Middle East, these unique childhood experiences proved invaluable to me.

One of my most vivid memories of West Point was the first day. It was hot and sunny and the upper classmen were waiting to get a hold of the new cadets.

Since I had attended Valley Forge Military Academy, I was well prepared. That evening when the new cadets marched out to Trophy Point and took the oath of allegiance, I thought to myself that I was proud to be following in my father's footsteps. Regrettably, my father died of cancer a few years after I graduated and he was not able to witness my military career.

As a military officer and leader, I loved leading my troops. They always came first and I sought out every opportunity to lead. Throughout my military career I was faced with many challenges, but I was always able to fall back on my West Point training. Years ago, I adopted two important rules that have served me well throughout my life: "When in command, take charge" and "Do what's right."

One of the real thrills of being a cadet is that everywhere you turn you find living history. The spirit and influence of the long, gray line is imbued in this campus and fortress. Enjoy the beauty of this book and the powerful words within. There is no other place quite like West Point and it is portrayed well within these pages. If you learn nothing else, remember those three important West Point words by which to live your life: "Duty, Honor, Country"-- duty with honor serving your country.

Cadets line up with precision, looking polished and distinguished. They are part of the new **LONG GRAY LINE** of soldiers. West Point has historically produced incomparable leaders who have served as Presidents, ambassadors, judges, cabinet members, educators governors, astronauts, engineers and CEOs. The young men and women pictured above will undoubtedly go on to fill those shoes well. At West Point they are given an unparalleled opportunity to mature intellectually, morally and physically in preparation for a rewarding and challenging career as an Army officer serving our nation.

INTRODUCTION

" The Hudson, that far famed, that beautiful river with its bosom studded with hundreds of snow sails. Again If I look another way I can see Fort Putnam frowning far above; a stern monument of a sterner age which seems placed there on purpose to tell us of the glorious deeds of our fathers and to bid us remember their sufferings and to remember their sufferings ---and to follow their examples." (Cadet Ulysses S. Grant, approximately 1840, from "The Generals"). General Grant had a poignant and accurate summary of West Point as a cadet.

Strategically located on the beautiful Hudson River, West Point is both an outstanding educational and military training institution in an imposing granite fortress with a rich and fascinating history. It is the oldest regularly garrisoned military post in America, occupied non-stop since January, 1778. During our country's fight for independence because of it's position on the Hudson, West Point was selected by General Washington as a defense position against British forces. Two years prior to Napoleon becoming Emperor of France, West Point was established in 1802, our nation's first engineering and military school. An integral part of our country's fabric prior to and since it's establishment two centuries ago, West Point started slowly compared to today: it first graduating class consisted of two cadets and it took until 1840 to boast 1,000 graduates. Today, West Point has trained and educated more than 64,000 young men and women with the highest academic, military and professional standards. West Point is highly regarded abroad for developing distinguished military leaders. It's graduates have had notable careers, serving during times of war and peace, fighting our battles in the War of 1812, the Indian Wars, the Mexican War, Spanish-American War, World War I, World War II, the Korean War, Desert Storm, as well as what some consider controversial wars, such as Vietnam and Iraq, where West Point graduates have served our country with duty and honor, doing their best under unimaginably distressful conditions. Most of the Class of 1846 fought in the Civil War, many became generals and a few are immortal. Graduates joined the side from where their root had sprung, and our nation was divided. After the Civil War, the Long Gray Line was instrumental in the healing of our nation's wounds and her reunification.

Indeed, the Long Gray Line of West Point is filled with some of the world's most distinguished leaders: Sylvanus Thayer, considered the "Father of the Military Academy," Robert E. Lee, Ulysses S. Grant, "Stonewall" Jackson, Douglas MacArthur, George S. Patton, Jr., Dwight D. Eisenhower, William C. Westmoreland, H. Norman Schwarzkopf and several astronauts: Edwin E. "Buzz" Aldrin, Edward White II and Michael Collins, to name a few.

The Academy's job is to train and educate young men and women, to develop their leadership skills so that they can take their place as commissioned officers in the army. Though West Point has mirrored our nation with many changes over the years, the beauty and mandate of the Academy remain the same, as does the essential constitution of this great institution. "Duty, Honor, Country" is the lifeblood of West Point. Whatever changes that may lie ahead, those ethics will be preserved and nurtured, for it represents all that is best about the U.S. Army.

It is the spiritual home of the Army's corps of officers and in this book, we hope that out of it's beautifully illustrated pages to capture with pictures and words the essence of this amazing historical military institution that has impacted so many lives: it's history, monuments, buildings, ethos and most important, its people. A motivating factor for creating this book is that most civilians have no idea of what goes on at West Point. West Point is a complex, constantly evolving and rich institution. We have only scratched the surface of all that is there and we encourage any reader to explore more of what West Point has to offer. We present a contemporary perspective of West Point and begin with a tour of the campus, then offer a glimpse into cadet life, an overview of academics, military instruction, athletics, commencement, a special chapter with pieces written by notable graduates and finally a look at the area surrounding West Point. It is our hope that all readers will come away with a vivid sense of what life is like at West Point for a cadet, from the first day that they arrive and experience the awe of living and learning in a fortress infused with 200 years of history, to the final joy of Graduation Day and becoming a commissioned officer. We thank West Point for the service given by her sons and daughters.

THE WASHINGTON MONUMENT is now positioned in front of Washington Hall looking out toward the Hudson River. It was originally on the northeast side of the Plain over by the Kosciuszko Monument and was moved to its present location in 1970. This large detailed equestrian statue of Washington, "Father of our Country" was sculptured by Henry Kirke Brown and unveiled in 1916.

HISTORY

West Point's critical part in the unfolding of our country's history dates back to the Revolutionary War (1775-1783), when the British and the Continental Army struggled to gain control over this strategic commanding plateau on the west bank of the Hudson River. The British strategy was to isolate New England and have their army from Canada meet up with their Army from New York. General George Washington, a fine leader, horseman and surveyor was the leader we needed. Realizing the British intent, Washington considered West Point to be the most important strategic position in America. It was a vital link between New England and the mid-Atlantic and the s-curve in the Hudson required sailing vessels to slow down to pass. Washington chose the Polish hero of the Saratoga War, Thaddeus Kosciuszko to capitalize on the geographic aspects of the Point that made it a desirable defense. Kosciuszko drew up the plans for the fortifications for West Point in 1778, and Washington shortly thereafter moved his headquarters to West Point in 1779. The Continental soldiers built batteries, forts and redoubts and extended a 150-ton iron chain across the Hudson to control river traffic. The chain was never put to test. Gun positions were located on Constitution Island and protected by redoubts on the nearby hills, and by Fort Arnold (later named Fort Clinton after Arnold's treason) on the plain of West Point. They succeeded in blocking the British from using the Hudson as a means of moving troops and supplies south. A General during the first 3 years of the Revolution, Benedict Arnold was behind a plot to sell the plans of the West Point Fortress. CAPT Andre was captured along with the note written by Arnold, but his capture was reported to Arnold who had time to obtain a boat and float down the Hudson to the British camp. George Washington would have rather exchanged Andre for Arnold and hung Arnold, but the British said no to the trade, so Andre was hung instead.

For three years the Continental Army dwelled in the hills of West Point and in 1783, the peace treaty was signed in Paris and America gained her freedom from the British.. Fortress West Point was never captured and became our country's first continuously occupied military post. In 1783, George Washington proposed a military academy for training army officers, but critics feared the creation of a military aristocracy and thought the idea was too European and undemocratic. Washington had supporters in Hamilton and John Adams who wanted to remove our reliance on foreign engineers and artillerists but it took two decades, until March 16, 1802 for Washington's idea to come to fruition. On that day, the United States Military Academy officially opened at West Point located on a commanding bluff overlooking the Hudson River, it was our nation's first engineering school.

Colonel Sylvanus Thayer, the "Father of the Military Academy," served as Superintendent from 1817-1833. He raised the academic standards, stressed honorable conduct and instilled military discipline. Civil engineering became the cornerstone of the curriculum and West Point graduates were mainly responsible for the construction of first bridges, roads, harbors, railroads, significant building and monuments and the Panama Canal.

West Point graduates began to fill the highest ranks and by the time of the Civil War, were leaders on both sides. Academy graduates, headed by generals such as Grant, Lee, Sherman and Jackson, were examples of fine military leaders for both the North and South. When the war ended, West Point grads were the first to lead the nation in a reconciliation.

The Spanish-American War in 1898 led to a larger regular army. Spurned by West Point graduates, after the Civil War, post-graduate command and staff schools and the Army National Guard were created. West Point now offered more than a strict civil engineering focus. In World War I, our forces were larger and West Point graduates were ready to take new war tactics, trench warfare, the enormous mobilization of troops, supplies and munitions. Academy graduates again distinguished themselves on the battlefield. It was a kind of war for which West Point grads were particularly adept. Large-scale American combat began 1918 and accelerated the final exhaustion of German reserves and the Armistice on November 11 that ended the war.

World War I severely disrupted West Point and after the war, Superintendent Douglas MacArthur brought her back to top performance by broadening curriculum, formalizing the Honor Code and made major changes in physical fitness requirements to prepare better soldiers. Eisenhower, MacArthur, Bradley, Patton and Stilwell were among a brilliant group of Academy graduates who rose to leadership in WWII. After the war, there were again extensive changes at West Point as a result of accelerating developments in science and technology and the recognition of the importance in understanding other cultures. In the early 1950's, West Point grads again rose to the task in keeping Communism at bay during the Korean War. Col. Joseph G. Clemons, commanded a company in 1953 in the infamous Korean War battle of Pork Chop Hill.

The Corps of Cadets grew in number as the result of President Johnson's visit to an Army-Navy game: before the game, the Naval Academy brigade marched onto the field and when it was Army's turn, the President is said to have remarked to the superintendent, "Where are the rest of your cadets?" Because the Army Reserves were so strong, West Point didn't need Brigade strength. But shortly after the game, President Johnson signed legislation in 1964 increasing the strength of the Corps of Cadets from 2,529 to 4,417 (more recently reduced to 4,000). To keep up with the growth of the Corps, a major expansion of facilities began shortly thereafter.

The end of the draft and the growing role of women and minorities brought about another major change at the Academy. In 1975 President Ford signed the law requiring the service academies to admit women and in 1976 the first women were brought to West Point as cadets.

In recent decades, the Academy's curriculum has evolved allowing cadets to major in any one of more than a dozen fields, including a wide range of subjects from the sciences to the humanities. West Point's focus continues to be meeting the needs of the Army and our country, and recognizing it must adapt in an ever-changing world. With it's long and noble history, West Point will continue to add officers imbued with "Duty, Honor, Country" to the incredible Long Gray Line.

AERIAL VIEW OF WEST POINT LOOKING WEST ACROSS THE HUDSON RIVER From the air you can get some idea of the immensity of West Point. The Hudson River flows from the north on the right to the south on left of the photo. "The Point" of West Point can be clearly seen in the photo. It is from the right side of the point that the chain going to Constitution Island was located. The Central Academic area is the light green area at the center of the Plain. The Thayer Gate and Buffalo Soldier Field are just outside this photograph on the left. Michie Stadium is by the Lusk Reservoir in the left-center of the photo. The road winding up through the middle of the photograph leads to Stony Lonesome Gate. The buildings on the far right side of the photo are the Garrison area. Route 9W is the small line in the trees across most of the top of the photograph.

THE CAMPUS

Located on a bluff in the Hudson Highlands, West Point is much more than a 16,000 acre military academy, it is a geological aberration and historic shrine of the American Revolution. First a military post under the command of Benedict Arnold, West Point was chosen as the best location by George Washington to prevent the British from sailing up the Hudson during the Revolutionary War. Washington selected this location due to it's unique and distinct geologic regions. The area's harsh topography resulted from various geological processes which kept it isolated until the discovery of it's significant iron ore deposits. The iron ore was the source of iron for the Great Chain that stretched across the Hudson to block the British ships during the Revolutionary War and was an important source of iron in the Civil War.

West Point rock is mostly granite and crystalline rock, which resists erosion by the powerful Hudson River. The river created a very deep river gorge out of the Highlands rock and three remarkably sharp turns in the river, one of which is at West Point. The river channel is even more narrow here because of Constitution Island, a rocky island directly north of West Point with independent mountain ridges on either side of the river gorge. From a military point of view the bluff is strategic, since at this point, the river is narrow and makes a hard turn, naval vessels and ships of the 1700's had to slow down to make the turn. The bluff and the Point's rolling topography also offers the advantage of being able to see clearly a long way up and down the Hudson.

West Point played a vital role in Washington's defeat of the British; the British ships didn't even make the attempt to pass the bluff where cannons could easily fire upon them from on high. After unsuccessful attempts to win the war in the North, the British turned to the South, and in 1781, British General Charles Cornwallis finally surrendered at Yorktown, Virginia.

West Point's location and geography have shaped America's history as well as the organization of this magnificent campus. The natural elements of the environment, the stone, river, valley and bluff have influenced the positioning and development of the architecture. Its founders looked to Europe's mistakes and accomplishments for direction and vision in its design. Even the architecture of West Point has an ominous importance and legacy that most architects could only dream of creating. The architecture is a blend of Gothic Revival and Greek Revival with the feel of a living granite fortress. Numerous glorious monuments offer testimony to West Point and American history.

In the pages that follow, we take you on a beautiful pictorial tour the campus starting with the Academic area, then the River Courts and Lower North Field, the Chapel area, Buffalo Soldier Area and finally the Garrison Area. As you will see, the thick, unmoving granite buildings compel one to think of the enduring spirituality of the "long grey line" as well as the beauty, history and tactical significance of this incredible institution.

Four thousand cadets march to **WASHINGTON HALL** three times a day and sit together for meals. Originally constructed in 1929, Washington Hall has a more unassuming look than the other campus buildings. The granite structure alludes to their style with its colossal center section, limestone carvings and notched spaces. The Washington Monument stands in front of Washington Hall guarding the edge of The Plain, a proper place for cadet reviews and parades.

14

Overlooking **WASHINGTON HALL** from on high is the Cadet Chapel. The additions to Washington Hall doubled the size of this imposing structure which houses many cadets, offices, classrooms, the dining space as well as the food prep area. Eight stories high in the center and six stories high on both wings, it also has additional facilities to accommodate those stationed at Camp Buckner who provide support to cadets during summer training.

15

The corps takes about five to six minutes to march into the dining wings of **WASHINGTON HALL**. The front of the old Washington Hall was preserved and has six dining wings emanating from it. The stained glass windows in the north wing depict the life of George Washington. An open balcony referred to as the "Poop Deck," is used by the Cadet Adjutant for making announcements and by the Superintendent, Commandant or Dean to entertain visiting dignitaries.

WASHINGTON HALL has a magnificent mural painted by artist Tom Lofton Johnson, *Panorama of Military History*. One of the largest inside seamless murals in the world, it covers more than 2,450 square feet of the south wall. The mural is the artist's visualization of historic military leaders and our country's 20 most decisive battles. General John J. Pershing unveiled the 70' long, 35' high painting in 1936.

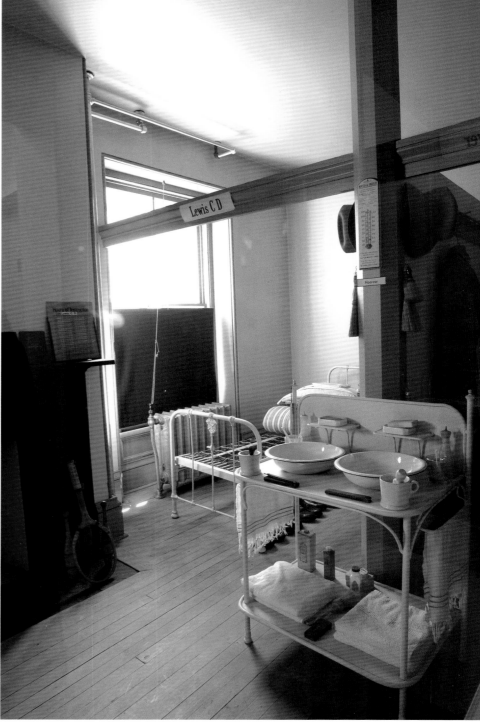

NININGER HALL, also known as the "Old Barracks," is not open to unescorted guests. There is not much left of the Old Barracks except Nininger, a small tower end-section which is used as offices and a museum. The museum rooms retain their original furnishings beginning when the time that the First Division lived here. Tower rooms were traditionally reserved for the highest ranking cadets such as John J. Pershing, Douglas MacArthur and H. Norman Schwarzkopf.

OLD CENTRAL BARRACKS

CADETS LINE UP IN FRONT OF L'ECOLE POLYTECHNIQUE MONUMENT

L'ECOLE POLYTECHNIQUE MONUMENT

Just outside of Nininger Hall is the Cadet Monument known as the **L'ECOLE POLYTECHNIQUE MONUMENT**. It is a replica of a statue standing on the grounds of the French military academy that bears the French Academy's name. Originally created as a tribute to the French cadets who took part in defending France in 1814, a replica was presented to West Point in 1919 as a gift from the French cadets in honor of West Point graduates who assisted in WWI.

The incredible view of the Hudson River Valley looking north from **TROPHY POINT** makes it a favorite place for cadets, alumni and visitors as history comes alive through the memorials commemorating our country's military conflicts. Located on the northern edge of the Plain, Trophy Point showcases captured war trophies since the Revolutionary War such as the cannons captured in the Battle of Saratoga and the War of 1812.

Located near Trophy Point, the **BATTLE MONUMENT** was dedicated in 1897 to soldiers of the Regular Army killed in the Civil War. A breath-taking sight and the largest piece of granite turned in the Western Hemisphere, this monument bears the names of 2,230 men inscribed on the memorial's ornaments. Crowning the monument is a statue of "Fame," a tribute to brave soldiers who have given their lives defending our freedom.

THAYER MONUMENT

DETAIL OF SEDGWICK MONUMENT

SEDGWICK MONUMENT IN FRONT OF BATTLE MONUMENT

The **THAYER MONUMENT** is inscribed, "Colonel Thayer, Father of the Military Academy." Sylvanus Thayer, Class of 1808, had the longest tenure as Superintendent, and the monument celebrates his many contributions to the Academy. The **SEDGWICK MONUMENT** was dedicated in 1868 to Major General John Sedgwick from the members of his last command. Cast from a cannon captured by the VI Corps which he commanded, rumor has it that an academically compromised cadet should go in full dress, under arms at midnight the night before the term-end examination and spin the rowels on the monument's spurs for luck. Hopefully, the cadet won't be seen.

DETAIL OF KOSCIUSZKO MONUMENT

VIEW FROM KOSCIUSZKO MONUMENT

KOSCIUSZKO GARDEN

KOSCIUSZKO MONUMENT LOOKING OUT ON THE HUDSON RIVER

The **KOSCIUSZKO MONUMENT** of Thaddeus Kosciuszko, a Polish artillery officer, was erected in 1828 by the Corps of Cadets. Kosciuszko was responsible for the turning point in the American Revolution, the victory at the Battle of Saratoga. He came to West Point in 1778 and spent two years designing and overseeing the construction of the formidable fortifications here. At the same time, he single-handedly designed and built his wonderful rock garden complete with a fountain that he built into the granite, which is located behind Cullum Hall.

23

MACARTHUR MONUMENT

EISENHOWER MONUMENT

MACARTHUR'S MEMORIAL, next to the MacArthur Barracks, was dedicated in 1969 by his wife, Jean. Douglas MacArthur, Class of 1903, returned to West Point 40 years after serving as Superintendent, and gave his famous, "Duty, Honor, Country" speech in 1962.   The **EISENHOWER MEMORIAL** is a nine-foot bronze statue of Dwight D. Eisenhower, Class of 1915, erected in 1983 on the southeast corner of the Plain.   It offers tribute to our nation's 34th President, General of the Army and the Supreme Commander of the Allied Forces in Europe during WWII.

AMERICAN SOLDIER STATUE

AIR CADET MEMORIAL

FLIGHT MEMORIAL

The **AMERICAN SOLDIER'S STATUE** was erected in honor of the American soldiers who gave their lives in battle and designed by the creator of the Iwo Jima Memorial, Felix Deweldon. The **AIR CADET MEMORIAL** was dedicated by the Corps in honor of cadets who gave their lives during flight training. The **FLIGHT MEMORIAL** is an eleven foot statue of an aviator rising on a column of flames and smoke and is dedicated to West Point graduates who have given their lives while in flight.

25

TAYLOR HALL THAYER AWARD ROOM

TAYLOR HALL ACADEMIC BOARD ROOM

TAYLOR HALL SUPERINTENDENT'S MEETING ROOM

An inside look at **TAYLOR HALL** offers a glimpse of it's splendor and vaulted Gothic Rooms. The **ACADEMIC BOARD ROOM** is lit by stained-glass windows emblazoned with the symbols of the Arts and Sciences. The impressive stone mantel is crowned by statues of the world's nine greatest heros. The **SUPERINTENDENT'S CONFERENCE ROOM** is equally striking, appointed by leather chairs, beautiful flags and the West Point and Corps of Cadets crests as is the **THAYER AWARD ROOM**, adorned by paintings of past Thayer Award recipients.

TAYLOR HALL

TAYLOR HALL is one of the world's highest all-stone masonry buildings. It has a 160' tower rising above Cullum Road at the heart of the Academy and embodies the spirit of the Academy with its rich ornamentation and grand stature. At the entrance are some of the various crests located around the building, the shields of the fifty states. Located within its walls are the USMA offices of Headquarters, Superintendent's Conference Room and the Thayer Award Room.

PERSHING BARRACKS (the former West Academic Building), was constructed in 1895 and modified into barracks in 1959 to accommodate the need for additional barracks. The building, named after General John J. Pershing, is rustic Massachusetts granite, lighter in color than other buildings. It's C-shape creates an important area behind the building known as "the area." Few cadets are unfamiliar with having to "walk the area."

DETAIL OF THAYER HALL FROM LOWER SOUTH FIELDS

DETAIL OF THAYER HALL

DETAIL OF THAYER HALL

VIEW OF THAYER HALL FROM LOWER SOUTH FIELDS

THAYER HALL was originally Riding Hall (built in 1911) and is one of the largest buildings at West Point. Riding instruction was abandoned in 1946, and in 1958 it was converted into an academic building. When looking across from the river or from the River Courts below, Thayer seems to rise out of the river valley. The Cadet Bookstore is located in Thayer Hall at the entrance level (4th floor) and welcomes visitors.

29

GRANT HALL EISENHOWER PORTRAIT

GRANT HALL

GRANT HALL DETAIL

GRANT HALL is the east wing of the Old South Barracks and was constructed in 1931 on the site where the cadet mess stood for nearly 80 years. Cadets holding rifles flank the main entry of the building named after President and General Ulysses S. Grant. The C-shaped building is used as a reception area for cadets and guests and contains paintings of America's five-star generals: Arnold, Bradley, Eisenhower, Marshall and MacArthur.

GRANT HALL DETAIL

GRANT HALL PAINTED BEAMS

QUIET MOMENT FOR CADET IN GRANT HALL

Art Deco style lettering adorns the entrance to **GRANT HALL.** The inviting Cadet Reception Hall is lavishly furnished and adorned with cleverly painted concrete beams made to look like wood. The beams have the insignia of the military divisions of WWI and the seals of the fifty states. The Cadet Restaurant is an equally welcoming place for cadets and visitors to socialize. The evolution of the Full Dress Hat is carved in stone over five of the windows.

31

MAHAN HALL

SCHWARZKOPF ROOM IN ADMINISTRATION BUILDING

MAHAN HALL

ADMINISTRATION BUILDING

MAHAN HALL with its towers on the south and north wings and sections that vary between four and six stories high, sustains the fortress like presence of West Point. Its granite facade merges well with the buildings nearby, and was originally designed to straddle Cullum Road to alleviate traffic. The **ADMINISTRATION BUILDING** started off as a large addition to the 1884 hospital and has been heavily modified since its completion in 1922.

LEE BARRACKS and Sherman Barracks are part of the New South Barracks constructed in 1962 on the site of the oldest wing of the hospital. The first story is set back on both the north and east sides for functional galleries. Lee Barracks faces Thayer Road and has the challenging task of blending with nearby buildings on Thayer Road. The high granite wall that faces the road has a dusting of petite windows that help set it apart.

WEST POINT CLUB

USMA LIBRARY

BARTLETT HALL

USMA LIBRARY

The **WEST POINT CLUB** was originally the Officer's Mess and Quarters. It's bright and magnificent dining room overlooks the Hudson River. **BARTLETT HALL** is an academic building named after Boyd Wheeler Bartlett, one of the original members of the National Academy of Sciences. It has subtle stone buttresses, large stone window trim connecting the top three floors and contrasting, recessed stone. The **USMA LIBRARY** continues the fortress theme of the campus with stylized buttresses which lend rhythm to the facade and arched Gothic windows. The symbol of the Academy, Athena, adorns the library tower. The facilities inside are vast and have everything a cadet could want for study and research.

CULLUM HALL, originally named Memorial Hall, takes its name from the Academy's sixteenth superintendent and it's first earnest historian. The exterior is of classical design, with pink granite, lions' heads along the cornice and massive bronze doors. The back of the building offers a wonderful view of the Hudson and steps down the slope to Kosciuszko's Garden. Inside is an assembly room and the hall displaying portraits of graduates and other memorabilia. The second floor is filled by the ballroom with its rich classical details, including 340 rosettes in the ceiling and substantial memorabilia.

RIVER COURTS WITH CREW BOAT HOUSE IN FOREGROUND

RIVER COURTS and south dock are where the crew house their boats. Called the Caulfield Crew and Sailing Center, this amazing facility provides space for Army Crew and Sailing operations, storage and maintenance. It is dwarfed by the imposing granite Mahan Hall and Thayer Hall above. New docks are just across the road from the new crew boat house.

AERIAL VIEW OF RIVER COURTS

LINCOLN HALL FROM THE RIVER COURTS

CADET ACTIVITY CLUB-OLD STATION

FLIRTATION WALK

The **RIVER COURTS** follow along the south bend in the Hudson River and give one a view of the academic area from the river. The **CADET ACTIVITY CLUB** was originally an train station, the preferred method of transportation to West Point for many years. It is a charming building with an octagonal chimney and luxurious interior. **FLIRTATION WALK** is a path used originally during the Revolutionary War to maintain the chain that went across the Hudson. The area is mostly out of sight of the Academy and became a popular place to meet visiting young ladies after 1840.

QUARTERS 100, THE SUPERINTENDENT'S HOUSE is the oldest structure that has been continually lived in at West Point. More than 10,000 people visit the house and garden each year. There has been considerable remodeling of the Federal-style structure which has been home to every superintendent since Sylvanus Thayer and has entertained almost every U.S. president. The front door, lock and key are the only thing original to the 1820 construction. In some ways this reflects the Academy itself which has been altered considerably over the years, but underneath are layers of history revered and kept very much alive.

GRANT ROOM

LEE ROOM

THAYER ROOM

DINING ROOM

Inside **THE SUPERINTENDENT'S HOUSE** the **GRANT ROOM** also known as the Music Room, features a portrait of Ulysses S. Grant and a grand electric player piano, circa 1930. A portrait of the 9th Superintendent, Robert E. Lee, is also the first thing you notice in the **LEE ROOM**. It is interesting that Lee is portrayed in his blue uniform "Union Suit." The **THAYER ROOM** is accented by a portrait of Colonel Sylvanus Thayer. In the **DINING ROOM** is an original signed Heppelwhite Sideboard and mahogany table and chairs, also Heppelwhite and were made to match the sideboard. The glass panels in the doors leading from the Music Room to the dining room won first place at the 1939 New York World's Fair.

GARDEN SUPERINTENDENT'S QUARTERS

The **SUPERINTENDENT'S GARDEN** has been a source of beauty to its residents and visitors since the Quarters were first occupied. Many varieties of plants and flowers from all 50 states as well as class trees are planted in the garden. The sundial was owned by Colonel Thayer and an enchanting gazebo is often used for musical interludes during garden receptions.

GARDEN SUPERINTENDENT'S QUARTERS

COMMANDANT'S QUARTERS (#101)

GARDEN SUPERINTENDENT'S QUARTERS

DEAN'S QUARTER'S (#102)

The **SUPERINTENDENT'S GARDEN** is made with the bricks of the original garden wall. The **COMMANDANT'S QUARTERS** was constructed at the same time as the Superintendent's and has always been home to the Commandant. It is also a Federal Style home which has been heavily renovated over the years. Next door is the **DEAN'S QUARTERS**, distinctly different in style than it's neighbors, reflecting the change in architectural taste to Gothic in the mid-1800's.

41

EISENHOWER HALL

EISENHOWER HALL

EISENHOWER HALL INTERIOR

ORDNANCE COMPOUND

EISENHOWER HALL is the Cadet Activities Center, or modern "student union," with a 4,500-seat auditorium, a 1,000-seat snack bar and cafeteria, a large ballroom, and other social rooms. Annually the theater hosts sixty major productions such as Broadway shows, musicals, jazz, rock and country music concerts. Located within the **ORDNANCE COMPOUND** is the Cadet Radio Station, Cadet Activity Club and the First Class Club. It is a significant historical site that dates back to the 1830's.

BAND BARRACKS

DIRECTOR OF HOUSING AND PUBLIC WORKS BUILDING

MILITARY POLICE BUILDING

AERIAL OF NORTH FIELDS AND GILLIS FIELD HOUSE

The **NORTH ATHLETIC FIELDS** are located below Eisenhower Hall and the Ordnance Compound. Here you will find the **BAND BARRACKS** with houses the Uniform Factory, Cadet Store and Band Facilities, the **MILITARY POLICE BUILDING** and the **DIRECTOR OF PUBLIC WORKS AND HOUSING**. The Softball and Football Complex as well as Gillis Field House with its state-of-the-art indoor track and field practice area, are also part of the North Athletic Fields.

The **CADET CHAPEL** is a symbol of religious activity at West Point and a famous landmark. The inside is a feast for the eyes, a play of light and color, rich with ornamentation, carvings and religious symbolism. The alter is carved from a single block of marble and the largest church organ in the world with 18,700 pipes is here. The magnificent stained glass sanctuary window is inscribed with the Academy's motto: "Duty, Honor, Country." The first pew railing has small silver plates engraved with the signatures of the previous Superintendents, such as General MacArthur and General William C. Westmoreland.

The **CADET CHAPEL** was built into the granite hillside and is constructed of native granite which blends nicely with it's surroundings. An Academy icon, it's architecture is that of a massive medieval fortress with Gothic themes which makes an impressive sight from the Plain below. It is a traditional cruciform building with a square tower and belfry complete with parapets. For years, cadet attendance at this Protestant chapel was mandatory. Regardless of the cadet's religion, the Cadet Chapel high on the hill was the official place of worship.

POST CHAPEL

JEWISH CHAPEL

JEWISH CHAPEL

After 20 years, the **JEWISH CHAPEL** was completed in 1984 and in 1986 the Jewish Chapel was deeded to the Academy. Made of the same native granite as the Cadet Chapel, similarities in construction end there. The Jewish Chapel has a vast Judaic collection and an exceptional library.   By early 1900's, it was clear that there would be two distinct areas at the Academy, the Academy and the post. The non-denominational chapel, the **POST CHAPEL** is not in the "Chapel Area." It is a simple, Georgian style building located in the Garrison area, covered in plain, red brick and dedicated in 1944.

The **CATHOLIC CHAPEL**, built in 1899 is the oldest house of worship in continuous use at the Academy. .
It also has the distinction of being the only structure on campus not owned by the government until 2000. The
chapel was built on a picturesque site offering an incredible sight from below and wonderful views of the
Hudson River. Also constructed of local granite and trimmed in limestone, it blends well with the rest of the
campus. The Chapel has a steeply pitched construction and a square bell tower on its east side.

CEMETERY CHAPEL WITH OLD ACADEMY GATES

CHAPEL INTERIOR VIEW

CHAPEL WITH ROBERT WEIR MURAL "WAR AND PEACE" OVER THE ALTAR

OLD CADET CHAPEL MOVED TO CEMETERY IN 1910

There was no regular chapel building until construction of the **OLD CADET CHAPEL** in 1836 making it the first house of worship at the Academy. A neoclassical design, the chapel was originally constructed in the central area, but when Bartlett Hall was scheduled to be built on that site in 1910, the alumni contributed funds to save their beloved chapel. It was dismantled stone by stone and reconstructed at its present site at the edge of the West Point Cemetery. Above the altar is a mural *War and Peace* and flanking the altar are 18 foot Corinthian columns. Here is Benedict Arnold's plaque, which has only his rank and date of birth; his name and date of death have been scratched out.

CARETAKER'S COTTAGE

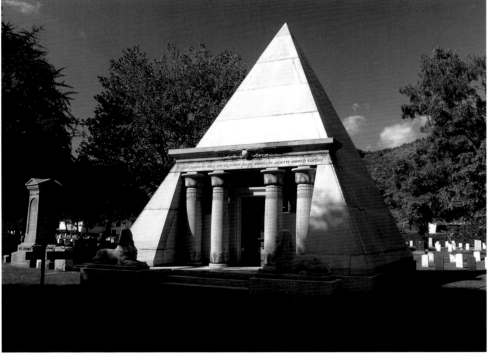

MAUSOLEUM FOR GENERAL EGBERT C. VIELE

MONUMENT TO GENERAL DANIEL BUTTERFIELD , AUTHOR OF "TAPS"

The **WEST POINT CEMETERY** sits on a promontory, once known as "German Flats," on Washington Road which overlooks the Hudson River and Constitution Island. There are more than 6,000 men and women buried here. The Egyptian-style mausoleum was designed by and has the remains of General Egbert C. Viele. General Daniel Butterfield is also buried here, author of Taps. Graves of past superintendents and many military, sports and civilian heroes rest here, such as Generals Custer, Thayer, Scott and Clay, a testimony to West Point history.

49

ARVIN CADET PHYSICAL DEVELOPMENT CENTER

ARVIN CADET PHYSICAL DEVELOPMENT CENTER

ARVIN CADET PHYSICAL DEVELOPMENT CENTER

LICHTENBERG TENNIS CENTER

LICHTENBERG TENNIS CENTER was completed in time for Army's 1999 winter/spring tennis season. One of the finest tennis facilities in the nation, it has a seven court arena, state of the art lighting and an elevated area for spectators. **ARVIN CADET PHYSICAL DEVELOPMENT CENTER** consists of six buildings constructed between 1910 and 1975. It is six stories and 455,000 square feet. West Point has a demanding physical development program, and a recent renovation has ensured that it has the facilities to keep pace with the demand placed on cadets.

KIMSEY ATHLETIC CENTER

MICHIE STADIUM

GROSS SPORTS CENTER

HOLLEDER CENTER

The new **KIMSEY ATHLETIC CENTER** was completed in 2002 and is on the south end of Michie Stadium. It features a state-of-the-art physical development facility. Dedicated to football, **MICHIE STADIUM** is one of the country's finest sports venues. It has the capacity to seat almost 40,000. The **GROSS SPORTS CENTER,** next to Lichtenberg Tennis Center, has a basketball court and one of the country's best gymnastics centers. The Army Gymnastics team has most of their competitions and practices here. **HOLLEDER CENTER** is located on the north side of Michie Stadium and houses Tate Rink, venue for Army ice hockey and Christl Arena for basketball.

HERBERT HALL, funded by alumni, is home to the Association of Graduates and is one of the newest buildings at the Academy. Located south of the Academic Area and Chapel Area, the brick building has nice stone details and numerous arches and gables. A dramatic paneled oval foyer with a balcony on the second floor creates an impressive entrance. The southern end of the building is a vast two-story hall for alumni gatherings broken into smaller, intimate spaces.

From **FORT PUTNAM** one can see the Hudson River Valley and most of West Point. One of several forts at West Point during the American Revolution, it was the main fortification for the network of redoubts and forts that made up West Point's defenses. From here, approaches to the Great Chain and the Plain could be protected from hostilities. Originally Fort Putnam was made of wood and earth redoubt but evolved into a stone fort which still stands. The exhibits at the West Point Museum describe the fort's critical role in our War for Independence.

BUFFALO SOLDIER FIELD GROUP

THAYER HOTEL

BUFFALO SOLDIER FIELD

BUFFALO SOLDIER FIELD GROUP

BUFFALO SOLDIER FIELD GROUP of buildings had designs for barracks and stables for the calvary stationed at West Point. Equestrian training was a fundamental part of cadet education until 1947. The former Calvary Stables now house offices and the former Artillery Stables now function as the Enlisted Men's Service Club and the Post Library. **THAYER HOTEL** is a wonderful addition to the campus very carefully sited and completed after 1903. It has hosted various important visitors, including Presidents Eisenhower, Kennedy, Nixon, Ford and Bush, who all stayed in the hotel's Presidential Suite.

WEST POINT VISITORS CENTER

ABRAMS GATE

THAYER GATE

WEST POINT VISITORS' CENTER is a part of the Buffalo Soldier area. The Visitors' Center attracts and informs the 3 million people that visit West Point each year. The buildings here are considerably separated by **THAYER GATE** as they were originally a part of the campus of Lady Cliff College. Thayer Gate Sentry Station is a rugged granite building with small towers that hints at the seriousness, history and architecture that lay beyond. The **ABRAMS GATE** is interesting in that it is not an Abrams tank but a Sherman Tank sitting on the wall of the gate, which is the tank that General Abrams commanded during WWII.

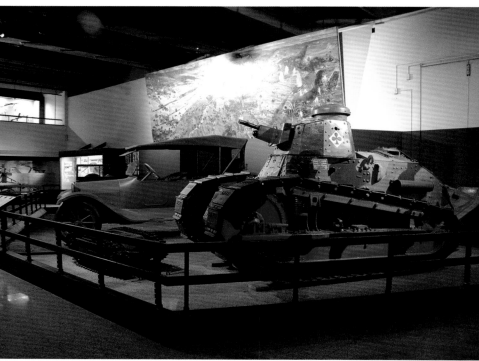

The **WEST POINT MUSEUM'S, OLMSTED HALL** collections represent all areas of West Point history and military study, from military art, objects and uniforms to artillery and cannons. Here are some of the most fascinating military artifacts and one of the best collections of military small arms in the country. A gallery portrays the history of our Army during peacetime and the Army's role as a nation builder. The museum also contributes its treasures to support the Department of History with exhibits in Thayer Hall which range from ancient to modern civilizations.

OLMSTED HALL , WEST POINT MUSEUM

The **WEST POINT MUSEUM** is located within **OLMSTED HAL**L. The area that includes the Visitors' Center is also known as the Pershing Center. Olmsted sits behind the rather plain Visitors' Center. Named after a major contributor to the museum, Major General George H. Olmsted, it is our country's oldest and largest military museum. With a majestic center tower and angled wings, this impressive piece of architecture was once a classroom building when it was part of Lady Cliff College.

KELLER HOSPITAL

GARRISON HOUSING

VICTOR CONSTANT SKI AREA

GARRISON HOUSING

The **GARRISON HOUSING** for enlisted men and women is architecturally plain but historically significant. **KELLER HOSPITAL**, located at the north end of post offers clinical services for cadets and other post personnel. The **VICTOR CONSTANT SKI SLOPE** is complete with facilities for skiers of all abilities. It has a chairlift, snow-making system, lodge and beginners' slope complete with rope tow. All three sites are part of the Garrison area.

HENRY WARNER HOUSE

BEAUTY OF ISLAND FROM THE DOCK

PART OF THE ISLAND WHERE THE GREAT CHAIN WAS FASTENED

HENRY WARNER HOUSE

CONSTITUTION ISLAND was the site of the first Revolutionary War fortification in this area. In 1777, the British overran the island but Americans returned in 1778 and made it part of Fortress West Point. It was purchased by Henry Warner in the 1830's and became home for his two daughters. The Warner House and fortifications such as the Great Chain still stand. It is available for pre-arranged tours and to cadets during time off. The island is a refuge place for the eagle, various creatures and 5,000 years ago, for Indians, which is evidenced by numerous Indian artifacts that have been excavated here.

CADETS MARCHING OUT OF WASHINGTON HALL

The transformation that takes place within the first six weeks is inspirational and a tribute to the Academy, its staff and the cadets. Moving in perfect unison, they are a beautiful sight to behold. At the heart of cadet life is The Cadet Honor Code: "A cadet will not lie, cheat, steal or tolerate those who do." This code is imbued into every cadet from the moment they arrive. The gray lines that exist outside of West Point are not to be crossed. Within this fortress, everything is either black or white and cadets police their own ranks.

CADET LIFE

Cadets arrive looking like normal teens but the transformation that takes place within one day is amazing. The change over four years is equally incredible as they mature into polished, well-trained and educated and honorable young officers devoted to duty. For the rest of their lives, they have a different walk, posture, demeanor and sense of pride that makes them easy to pick out from among a crowd of civilians. The first day, Reception Day (R-Day), is forever etched into the memory of every cadet. After two or three minutes for saying goodbye to family, the new cadets are shuttled to an imposing building with thick steel doors twice a cadet's height, which close behind each group of cadets with a mysterious finality. As the day goes on, individuality slowly slips away and being a part of a group takes on a somewhat confusing but ominous significance.

Being a new cadet and after the first six weeks, a plebe, mandates group activity. The entire day is structured around military decorum and succeeding in just about anything here requires that cadets learn to think of themselves as part of a group where everyone must succeed. This is in stark contrast to the usual "may the best man win" attitude at most colleges. The upperclass cadets immediately begin instructing new cadets in the finer points of cadet life, such as how to salute, dress properly, what to say and of course, march. This first summer distinguishes those who are able to fail and persevere. Moments of solitude are relished and rare: virtually every moment is spent in the company of others, marching, running, studying, eating, training, testing, showering, sweating; a first year cadet is never alone. They are in the Army now and the Army owns their time.

As part of the Regular Army, a cadet is paid a small stipend and receives Army benefits in addition to room, board and tuition. Cadets pay for their uniforms, textbooks, computers and other expenses out of their stipend. The attitude and professionalism associated with the Army permeates all aspects of life here. This is no college town. Drugs and alcohol are not tolerated and there is unannounced and routine testing, including when cadets return from leave. A cadet that tests positive is dismissed, period, end. Due to their training and the Cadet Honor Code, there is virtually no theft and everyone is courteous, even when no one is looking. This is one of the few college campuses where you could leave a $100 bill on the table and come back and find it later.

The Corps of Cadets consists of about 4,100 men and women pursuing military training and an undergraduate education culminating with a commission in the Army. Their ranks are similar to the Army's in order to develop leadership skills and the upperclass Corps of Cadets is responsible for running the entire brigade. Fourth Class cadets or freshmen hold the rank of private, Third Class cadets or sophomores are corporals, Second Class or juniors are sergeants and the First Class cadets, seniors are officers. There are 32 cadet companies each consisting of 4 platoons with 4 squads each, with a squad consisting of 7-10 cadets. A battalion is comprised of 4 companies each, the regiments have 2 battalions each and the Corps or brigade, which consists of 4 regiments. Third Class cadets (second-year) serve as Team Leaders for each squad, personally supervising one or two first-year or Fourth Class cadets. Third-year or Second Class cadets serve as cadet noncommissioned officers overseeing the lower two classes of cadets. Fourth-year or First Class cadets fill the roles of First Captain, Regimental Commanders, Battalion Commanders, Company Commanders and Platoon Leaders and other staff positions. The Honor Captain and the Respect Captain are First Class cadets that assist the Brigade staff with ethical and honor issues among the Corps.

Besides it's own chain of command, the Corps is overseen by the Brigade Tactical Department which is led by an active duty Colonel in the position of Brigade Tactical Officer. Each of the four regiments is commanded by a Regimental Tactical Officer who is a Lieutenant Colonel. Each cadet company is overseen by the Company Tactical Officer, a Major or a Captain as well as a Company Tactical Noncommissioned Officer, a Master Sergeant or Sergeant First Class. Within the Brigade Tactical Department is the Center for Personal Development, an accredited counseling center for cadets. The purpose of this team of officers is to develop, inspire and support cadets through all aspects of their lives at the Academy. They are available to cadets everyday, from reveille until taps and attend military training, ceremonies, drill practice and sports with their cadet companies. They are also the point of contact for parents and staff for any matter or question about a cadet. The Center for Professional Military Ethic is a part of the Brigade Tactical Department which assists in developing cadet character, promotes the Cadet Honor Code and "The 7 Army Values" Loyalty, Duty, Respect, Selfless Service, Honor, Integrity and Personal Courage. All of this is done over a four year period and includes 44 classroom hours of progressive instruction in Honors education.

When cadets aren't busy with all of their requirements, they have many other activities they can be involved in. There are numerous clubs, from chess to glee club to ballroom dancing, sports clubs to military clubs like the pistol club and parachuting. Mentors of the West Point Mentor Program are West Point Officers who are married and live on Post and open their homes to cadets when they have free time so that they can enjoy some of the comforts of family life and relax. Religion is another important but no longer mandatory aspect of cadet life. Eisenhower Hall offers cadets a chance to see touring companies like Camelot and performers such as Elton John. Dances or "Hops" are hosted by Eisenhower almost every weekend. The transformation from the eager new cadet to inspiring officer is a complicated passage and cadet life is rewarding but sometimes hectic and harsh. But out of that harshness incredible bonds are formed amongst cadets, cadets and officers, and cadets and enlisted officers. Most graduates would relish the chance to return to West Point and many do.

In stark contrast to civilian college students, cadets surrender a number of their individual rights. From the time the oath is taken by cadets on R-Day, they lose the right to decide where they will live and work, how they dress, wear their hair and what they will do during the summer. These restrictive regulations are essential to military discipline, to the smooth functioning of a unit under the situations more formidable than most civilians could begin to imagine. Cadets are training to defend Democracy but do not, themselves, live democratically unless they leave the army after the mandatory five years of service; they surrender these rights so that we may enjoy them. It is a fascinating balancing act most civilians do not consider between individual freedom and the unavoidable practicalities of military service. Our democratic society values individual rights above all else, while the military culture is founded on the subordination of the individual to the group as it is not an individual soldier who wins a war, but a military unit. The truly wonderful part of this scenario is that these teens make a conscious choice to give up these rights in order to serve our country. But what they give up is not without its rewards as all of their basic needs are met, they have excellent benefits, an incredible education and opportunity for further graduate education, form incomparable deep and enduring friendships, fare well professionally and are living the admirable passion they have for selfless service to our country.

WAITING IN LINE TO BE PROCESSED

"YOU ARE IN THE ARMY - NOW! GET IN LINE."

GOODBYE TO FRIENDS AND RELATIVES

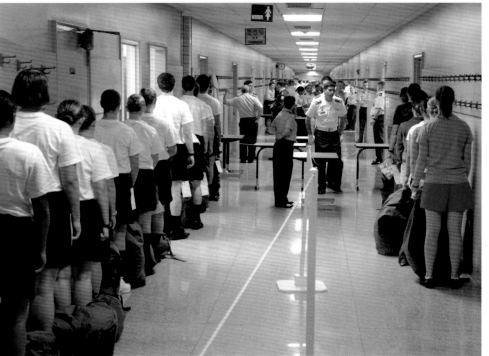

GETTING MEDICAL EVALUATIONS

Cadets quickly learn that they have left civilian life behind. After a pleasant farewell to family and friends, they are assigned their quarters, are responsible for staying with their company, get medical evaluations, inoculations, are issued their clothes and uniforms. The pressure cooker starts on **RECEPTION-DAY** (R-Day) and continues at high pressure through the first six weeks of Cadet Basic Training. Once the rest of the cadre returns from summer training, the pressure continues to rise through the next nine months for the new plebes. The incoming cadets think that plebe year is a type of rite of passage to separate the wheat from the chaff. It will take some time before they realize that their assumption is incorrect.

PLEBES GETTING NEW UNIFORMS

OFFICIAL OATH WITH A SIGNED COPY

"WHAT IS YOUR NAME? ADDRESS ME AS SIR"

THE NEW HAIR STYLE

On **R-DAY** new cadets learn that each company is run by a First Class cadet. Appropriately addressing an officer is mandatory as is a proper haircut, proper salutations, etc. The day goes quickly as they get their new uniforms, sign the official oath and within hours of their arrival, new cadets better know how to answer "New cadet, what are your four responses?" From this day on, cadets are on the go from reveille at 6:30 a.m. until 11:30 p.m. when they must be in the barracks for taps. They shine their shoes, clean their room every day, stand inspections, wear a proper uniform everywhere, and have to do it all correctly.

ONE OF A HUNDRED "LINE UPS" DURING THE DAY

THE DAYS NOT OVER YET

WHAT'S YOUR NAME PLEBE, GET YOUR TOES OFF MY LINE

ARE YOU LOOKING AT ME PLEBE

Beginning on **R-DAY**, cadets are conditioned to do routine things routinely. Upperclassmen implement the Leadership Development System with a firm but hands-off approach. As a visitor, one frequently hears a stern "New cadet, step up to my line. Not on my line but up to my line." The conflict that seems to develop between incoming cadets and upperclassmen is a result of bad habits or attitudes a new cadet must change to succeed. New cadets arrive knowing they are the best of the best and are used to praise; one attitude that will need changing in many new cadets is that of arrogance. To see more on Cadet Basic Training, see the chapter on the Department of Military Training.

MEMORIZING THE "BUGLE NOTES"- REQUIRED READING

TROPHY POINT OATH

FORMAL OATH OF ALLEGIANCE, AT TROPHY POINT

FORMAL END OF A REAL LONG DAY

Bugle Notes is required reading, in fact, cadets are expect to know it cover to cover. It is in some ways the cadet bible and key to survival as it contains information on West Point history, physical requirements, general military information, cadet rank information on buildings, monuments and facilities, etc. By the end of Reception-Day, about one percent of the incoming have quit. An uplifting end to an exhausting day, every member of the Long, Gray Line has survived this day to take the **OATH OF ALLEGIANCE** shown above at Trophy Point. They are officially in the Army now and have pledged allegiance to uphold the Constitution of the United States.

MALE CADET ROOM

FEMALE CADET ROOM

FEMALE CADET ROOM

NON-COMISSIONED OFFICER COUNSELING A CADET

Though they are called barracks, **CADET DORMITORIES** are much like those at any civilian college with two to three cadets per room. They live with cadets from their company and the room is equipped with wireless access for their laptops and a private phone line on each desk. The rifle and uniform remind cadets that this is not any ordinary college. The company non-comissioned officer is seen above counseling a cadet. A non-comissioned officer is assigned to each company and offers opportunities for cadets to learn from them about life as a soldier as well as respect for non-comissioned personnel. On graduation day, this non-comissioned officer will proudly salute his former charge as a new officer.

Above a **COMPANY COMISSIONED OFFICER,** part of the Brigade Tactical Department, is counseling a cadet officer, a Firstie. He is responsible for the success of the officers in the Corps of Cadets. In the picture is a goalpost the enlisted officer found laying outside, waiting to be discarded after a football game. He has kept it as a West Point souvenir and memento of fun times. "I love you" is written on the chalkboard in the background. The officer's wife and children left him these messages as he is readying to report for duty in Kuwait.

67

FULL DRESS GRAY OVER WHITE UNIFORM   FULL DRESS GRAY OVER WHITE UNIFORM

The **FULL DRESS GRAY OVER WHITE UNIFORM** pictured above is worn at very formal summer occasions, such as graduation. Cadets at West Point spend the majority of their time some type of uniform and there is a different uniform for just about every activity of a cadet's day. Cadet gray came about in 1814 when the government was unable to furnish troops with blue material. The color was adopted in 1815 to commemorate General Jacob Brown's victory over the British at Chippewa in July of 1814.

FULL DRESS GRAY UNIFORM

CADET WHITE UNIFORM

The **FULL DRESS GRAY UNIFORM** was adopted in 1816 and has remained the same throughout the years. This is the winter uniform worn to very formal events and is the equivalent to a civilian tuxedo. The Full Dress Hat also known as the "tarbucket," is worn with the Full Dress Coat for formal dress parades and ceremonies. The **CADET WHITE UNIFORM**, also known as "India White", has been at West Point since 1886 and is the warm weather alternative to the Full Dress Gray. Redesigned in 1959, the current white uniform is worn primarily for social events during the spring, summer and fall.

FEMALE DRESS MESS UNIFORM

WHITE OVER GRAY UNIFORM

The **FEMALE DRESS MESS** is for formal occasions and celebrations such as hops and banquets in lieu of the Full Dress Gray. No caps or hats are required for women in Dress Mess. The **WHITE OVER GRAY UNIFORM** is less formal and worn during the summer. Whenever a cadet is outside, a hat or cap must always be worn.

Traditionally, cadets wore their dress gray uniform trousers and a gray flannel shirt to class. In 1947, the **AS FOR CLASS UNIFORM** of gray flannel was replaced with a tropical worsted wool shirt. Since that time it has been worn with the dress gray trousers as the regulation class uniform. A tie accompanies the winter shirt. This is the uniform seen most frequently at West Point during the academic year.

DRESS GRAY UNIFORM

ATHLETIC UNIFORM

Pictured above is the **DRESS GRAY UNIFORM**. In 1889, the gray blouse, trimmed down the front, around the bottom and up the back with black mohair braid one inch wide, was adopted to replace the gray shell and riding jackets. This same coat is worn today as a semi-dress uniform with either white or gray trousers. In addition to the purely cadet uniforms, cadets also wear uniforms that are utilized Army-wide like the athletic uniform for physical workouts and games called **GYM A**. It consists of a gray t-shirt and black gym shorts.

ACU'S, ARMY COMBAT UNIFORM

ARMY COMBAT UNIFORM

Cadets wear **ARMY COMBAT UNIFORM or ACU's** for field training, rallies before a football game and other functions. A hat accompanies this uniform which is like the active-duty Army uniform. Throughout the month of July, cadets schedule several fittings at the uniform factory. They receive most of their uniforms during their plebe year. After initial alterations, cadets can have any item repaired, or have patches and service stripes, etc. added on at the factory during their 4 years here.

Like the Full Dress Coat, the long, gray overcoat pictured above is still hand-made at the **CADET UNIFORM FACTORY.** Much of the Academic year, a heavy overcoat is needed as the winters can be harsh. Official overcoats were adopted by Thayer in 1828. Copied by military schools around the country, it is a customary part of a cadet's uniform. The skilled tailors make these coats by hand much in the same way as their predecessors did over 150 years ago. Cadets learn to appreciate the importance of their uniforms and looking sharp after graduation. Many retain life-long habits of neatly pressed clothes and shined shoes.

WEST POINT FOOD PREPARATION

UNITED STATES MILITARY ACADEMY BAND

WEST POINT'S FOOD PREPARATION

UNITED STATES MILITARY ACADEMY BAND

WEST POINT'S FOOD PREPARATION has incredible organization and a dedicated staff to serve 7.8 million meals annually to over 4,000 hungry West Point cadets. The food preparation area is vast and high-tech and is not normally seen by the public. The **UNITED STATES MILITARY ACADEMY BAND** selects soldiers who have attended the nation's best music schools. It is the Army's oldest active band and dating back to the Revolutionary War, it is the oldest unit at West Point. It has a Concert Band, the Hellcats (drum and bugle field unit) and the Jazz Knights which fulfill all of the official musical needs of the Academy.

COMBAT WEAPONS TEAM

WKDT RADIO STATION

INFANTRY TACTICS CLUB

GOSPEL CHOIR

The **COMBAT WEAPONS TEAM** is a club offered by the Department of Military Instruction (DMI). Cadets become versed in using a rifle, pistol and shotgun and learn skills necessary in urban warfare and close quarters combat. The **INFANTRY TACTICS CLUB** is another DMI Club designed to enhance leadership skills as well as tactical and technical expertise in light infantry training. **WKDT RADIO STATION** is an FM station run by cadets in operation since 1956 that supports the Corps and the local community with hard work and volunteered time. Established in 1976, the **GOSPEL CHOIR** offers cadets an opportunity to sing with a choir for West Point Community Service.

WEST POINT SPECIAL OLYMPICS

GEN SCHWARZKOPF REVIEWS CENTER FOR ENHANCED PERFORMANCE

WEST POINT SPECIAL OLYMPICS

CENTER FOR ENHANCED PERFORMANCE

Shown above is one of several annual events hosted by West Point, the Orange County Spring Games for **SPECIAL OLYMPICS**. A cadet is assigned to every special athlete and is responsible for getting the athlete to and from their events. Cadets boost the morale of the athletes and as the day passes, special bonds are formed. The **CENTER FOR ENHANCED PERFORMANCE** offers cadets instruction in applied performance technology. Using state-of-the-art methods and technologies such as biofeedback, they train cadets to be able to focus, have confidence and composure when under pressure or in the midst of distractions or stress. It is useful to cadets in all aspects of West Point life, athletics, academics and military training.

Pictured above, a cadet applies what he has learned in the **DEPARTMENT OF CHEMISTRY AND LIFE SCIENCES** one of 13 Academic Departments. The curriculum design has been modified many times over the years in order to achieve it's mandate to serve the needs of the Army and in setting academic standards of excellence. Physical sciences and engineering are balanced with the humanities and social sciences to lay the groundwork for commissioned officers to lead our Army forward into the 21st century.

ACADEMIC PROGRAMS

Getting into West Point is a bit like going through the obstacle course at Camp Buckner. In addition to the normal SAT, essays and teacher recommendations, the process requires three additional steps. The first is a complete physical, then a six-event physical fitness test and finally a candidate must be nominated by a member of Congress or the Vice President. West Point is both an excellent military training institution as well as an outstanding academic college, providing breadth and depth in its curriculum. In a typical year, around 12,000 students apply to West Point out of which around 1,200 are accepted, representing all 50 states and some foreign nations. A potential cadet must be academically and physically qualified and demonstrate leadership abilities. Of the ones who are accepted, approximately 75% are in the upper 20% of their graduating high school class and half score above 600 on both the math and verbal SAT, with almost one quarter scoring above 700 on each. This is compared to an average score of 520 and 510 on math and writing respectively which is acceptable for most colleges. About 80% of those admitted are members of the National Honor Society and over 1,000 are Varsity Letter Winners. West Point and Princeton University are the only colleges in the country that rank in the top four for both the Rhodes and the Hertz Scholarships that are awarded for excellence in academics.

The core curriculum at West Point offers 31 courses well balanced between the arts and sciences and has 22 optional majors and 25 different fields of study. All cadets are required to take at least three courses in calculus and three in engineering. They choose their majors during their second year, in the fall and up until the third year, they all take the same courses. It provides the background and breadth of knowledge needed by an Army officer. As one reads the goals of the various academic departments, it is clear that they all have the common goal of educating, motivating and developing Army officers of character prepared to serve our nation. Cadets are encouraged to participate in class daily, are supported in self-directed learning and are evaluated frequently. If unsure of the material taught on any given day, or if one desires to move beyond the material, extra one-on-one instruction is available. The present curriculum reflects more than 195 years of evolutionary change both in the military professional education and in higher education. Today's balanced offering of courses leads to a Bachelor of Science degree because of the engineering requirements and builds a foundation for continuing education and professional development. Approximately 80% of West Point graduates who remain in the Army beyond their initial commitment do attend graduate school, usually funded by the Army. Cadets can major in Behavioral Sciences and Leadership,

Chemistry and Life Science, Civil and Mechanical Engineering, Electrical Engineering and Computer Science, English, Foreign Languages, Geography Environmental Engineering, History, Law, Mathematical Science, Physics, Social Sciences or Systems Engineering and those who have outstanding records in their majors may be invited to participate in challenging honors programs. Each year West Point cadets compete for and win many prestigious scholarships. As of 2007, West Point was 4th on the list of total winners for Rhodes Scholarships, 7th for Marshall and 4th on the list of Hertz Fellows.

At West Point, a cadet is far more than a mere face in the crowd. Classes are small, usually 12 to 18 cadets to insure individual participation and individual attention. The faculty here is the cream-of-the-crop and very invested in their young charges. Military professors make up about 80% of the faculty. This is sometimes seen as both an asset and a deficit. Civilian professors are usually a permanent part of the West Point scene which lends to continuity. On the other hand, Military professors offer cadets insight into their personal military experiences but frequently get assigned to a new position. Both military and civilian professors are committed to the success of each and every cadet. They model Army values and inspire cadets to serve our nation with both expertise and allegiance. The faculty are very involved in cadet life and act as coaches, tutors, club advisors and participate in other extra curricular cadet activities. Most of the faculty lives on post and is very immersed in the West Point community. This is in stark contrast to other colleges where professors leave the campus as soon as they are able.

More is required of a cadet to graduate than from a civilian college student. They have to successfully complete 40 academic courses that are a minimum of 3 credit hours each, successfully complete eight military science courses that are 3 credit hours each, successfully finish summer training each year and meet the requirements of Physical Education under the Office of the Commandant. West Point has the resources to provide outstanding facilities, technology and equipment, and the staff to further cadet learning. Clearly, West Point cadets are the best of the best and the West Point learning environment is head and shoulders above most. When they arrive at West Point, these teenagers have an advantage compared to many college students. They have already demonstrated leadership, community service, intelligence, physical fitness, adaptability, are knowledgeable and are willing to forgo all that makes a civilian college appealing to teens.

The **DEPARTMENT OF PHYSICS** teaches preferred courses in the fields of physical science and nuclear engineering with the underlying intent of preparing cadets to consider the technical aspects of problem solving in the field. Some of the department's objectives are to teach cadets the basic laws of physics, how to apply them, to apply the scientific method, to be able to communicate findings discernibly and succinctly, to learn practical application of skills learned in other courses such as chemistry and math, and to develop logical and abstract thinking and systematic problem solving.

Pictured above is one of several examples of ongoing individual research projects conducted by **DEPARTMENT OF PHYSICS** cadets and staff with practical application for the Army. Cadets in all departments can participate in independent research, instruction and studies, often hand-in-hand with another agency. Pictured above, a cadet is working with an Army Research Lab in Maryland in the area of photonics. The objective is to find an opaque dye unaffected by lasers that could be eye and sensor protection for soldiers in the field.

The **DEPARTMENT OF GEOGRAPHY & ENVIRONMENTAL ENGINEERING** provides cadets with an understanding of the natural world and its people and their interaction with the best facilities available. The department offers instruction in Environmental Engineering, Environmental Science, Geospatial Information and of course, Environmental Geography and Human Geography. With increasing international security interests, all of these areas are crucial to the needs of the Army in providing security for our nation.

The **DEPARTMENT OF ELECTRICAL ENGINEERING AND COMPUTER SCIENCE** offers 3 areas of study including Information Technology. The department has 30 high-tech labs available to cadets and is always planning for the future in designing its programs. The IT program fulfills the Army's need for officers who can quickly configure and mesh together large collections of new and existing equipment in the field. Electrical Engineering teaches cadets to see a project through to completion by learning basic skills and focusing on a particular area of study. Cadets have the opportunity to learn in areas such as robotics and computer architecture in top-notch facilities.

83

The **DEPARTMENT OF MATHEMATICAL SCIENCES** recognizes that cadets enter West Point with a variety of backgrounds in math. Cadets are taught to be capable and assured in problem solving and develop the skills needed to succeed in courses needed in other departments that rely heavily on math abilities. All cadets are required to take 3 levels of Calculus and a course on Probability and Statistics. The department strives to instill in cadets abilities in mathematical reasoning, mathematical modeling, history of math, scientific computing and communication.

The **DEPARTMENT OF LAW** does not train cadets to be lawyers or to know a body of legal knowledge. The study of law requires a perspective on history and culture as well as an awareness and ability to solve moral and ethical problems. It leads to a better understanding of how individuals, organizations and societies obtain their objectives and develops a cadet's critical thinking abilities. The focus is on creating tomorrow's leaders in a changing and sometimes uncertain world.

The **DEPARTMENT OF HISTORY** teaches American, Military, European, Strategic and International History. Show above is a class on Military History with weapons on display for cadets to investigate which are on loan from the West Point Museum. Military History looks at all aspects of warfare from Medieval times to present modern-day warfare. Instruction in the science and strategy of military art was within the Department of Civil and Military Engineering until 1923, except for a brief period in 1864. In 1969, the department became independent and is one of West Point's largest departments.

The **DEPARTMENT OF ENGLISH** has several goals that go way beyond basic English. It aspires to teach cadets to organize and express thoughts coherently and precisely and to assist them in becoming more reflective and aware of the importance of examining one's life with an understanding of philosophy and moral discourse. The department also seeks to instill a love of literature and creativity as well as appreciate the cultural diversity in our country and world.

Established by the direction of General Dwight D. Eisenhower, the **DEPARTMENT OF BEHAVIORAL SCIENCES AND LEADERSHIP** offers majors in engineering psychology, leadership, management, psychology, and sociology. Pictured here, engineering psychology cadets study the human nervous system to better understand the role of the brain in human behavior.

The **DEPARTMENT OF BEHAVIORAL SCIENCES AND LEADERSHIP** focuses on developing an understanding of the scientific basis of human behavior and of the psychological and social components of effective leadership. Pictured here, a leadership instructor leads a discussion on the finer points of leading Soldiers in combat.

The **DEPARTMENT OF SYSTEMS ENGINEERING** offers five different program majors. One of those programs is shown here, Systems Engineering. Systems Engineering is the art and science of making decisions in evolving and complex environments and is a rapidly growing field with applications in the military and private sector. An Abrams tank can be thought of as a system. Its components, the driver, gunner, armament, computer system, gas turbine engines, etc. must all function together in order to successfully complete an Army mission. There are systems throughout society, not just in the military, such as our food supply system or transportation system. Systems engineers work to make these systems more efficient, more cost effective and longer lasting.

The **DEPARTMENT OF SYSTEMS ENGINEERING** uses simulation, modeling and information systems to teach cadets how systems work and to be expert problem solvers as systems engineers. The department also has a program in Information Engineering that looks at how information is transmitted, used and stored in a rapidly evolving technology. The Engineering Management program is multidisciplinary instruction in finance, accounting, leadership, engineering and management. Systems Management studies defense acquisition, design and management systems while considering budget, schedules and performance needs. Operations Research is a program handled in conjunction with the mathematics department.

The **DEPARTMENT OF CIVIL AND MECHANICAL ENGINEERING** has a variety of labs for cadet learning such as a concrete lab, wind tunnel, soils lab, turbine lab, automotive labs, fluid lab and vibrations lab. Civil Engineering requires that cadets are capable in various disciplines within Civil Engineering, such as hydro, environmental, structural and geotechnical engineering. They are expected to be able to design civil engineering systems and components, to be creative in solving engineering problems and consider the social, political, technological, ethical and economic aspects of the problem.

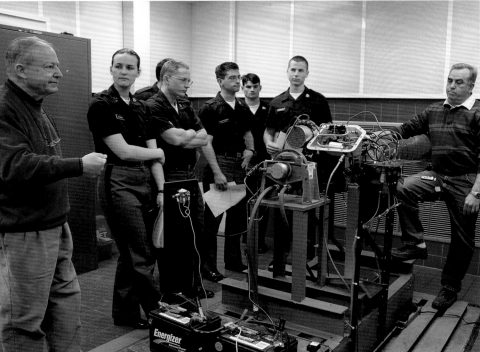

The **DEPARTMENT OF CIVIL AND MECHANICAL ENGINEERING** requires that cadets be proficient in areas of math, chemistry, physics and higher math such as multivariate calculus in order to solve engineering problems. In Mechanical Engineering, they are expected to be able to design thermal and mechanical systems, conduct experiments, interpret data and communicate effectively. With a focus on modern engineering tools and issues that effect engineering problem solving, the intent is to meet the mechanical engineering needs of the Army and our country.

OPERATION HIGHLAND WARRIOR is part of summer training at Camp Buckner. This is no leisurely hike through the woods. The cadet shown above is carrying about 40 pounds of equipment on his back and wearing his helmet most of the day while scouting in the summer heat through thick woods, complete with bugs and underbrush . Not what your average civilian teen would be doing. Summer training manuevers may look like fun to the outsider, but it is physically and mentally pushing cadets beyond their imagined limits.

DEPARTMENT OF MILITARY INSTRUCTION

Beginning on Reception Day until the day West Point grads leave the Army, military training is an inseparable part of their lives. At West Point, military training is all pervasive and year-round but the majority of the hands-on training takes place during the summer. The motto of the Department of Military Instruction (DMI) Is "We bring the Army to the classroom." They do that quite literally with a complex, well organized department that hosts prominent guest lecturers, exchanges, thorough academic year instruction which is integrated with summer training and state-of-the-art facilities. They train the Corps of Cadets in the fine points of warfare, the Profession of Arms and make the transition from civilian to cadet and commissioning officer progressive and smooth. To keep up with the pace of a rapidly changing world and the Army's needs, DMI continually revises its military training. Every instructor in DMI is a model soldier and officer, teaches by example and participates by leading cadet summer training.

DMI has several divisions all of which complement each other: the Military Training Branch, Military Science, Cadet Leadership Development, Cadet Branching, Cadet Military Clubs and events rounded out with Professional Military Ethic. In Military Training (MT), the MT officers oversee all aspects of cadet summer training as well as First Class Branching experiences, the Sandhurst Cup Competition and any branch mentoring programs. During the summer, all four classes of cadets experience difficult and realistic hands-on military training. Cadet Basic Training (CBT) transitions civilian teens to cadets with the traditional military courtesies and skills they need to become physically fit team players capable of following orders. CBT is a six-week program that physically and mentally challenges new cadets. A series of foot marches, rifle marksmenship, 75-foot rappels, hand-to-hand combat, map reading, small unit tactics, throwing live grenades, donning gas masks and walking through the "house of tears" and bayonet fighting techniques are just some of the skills new cadets learn. Their six week training culminates with a 24-hour exercise where cadets work together in squads and apply the skills they've learned. CBT ends with new cadets marching 15 miles back to the main post. After successful completion of CBT, new cadets officially become plebes during the Acceptance Parade Ceremony.

Cadet Field Training (CFT) is seven weeks of military training at Camp Buckner which gives Third Class cadets an introduction to close ground fighting, light and mechanized, in a tactical environment. Training is designed to push cadets mentally and physically to give all they've got and then give more. The capstone event of CFT is Operation Highland Warrior where cadets carry out live fire ambushes, communicate by tactical radios, process captives, conduct cordon and search, check point and other defensive operations. Their training ends with a week of Mounted Maneuver Training in Fort Knox, Kentucky, where they're exposed to the Calvary branch and the Army's most lethal weapons.

During their last two summers at West Point, cadets complete Cadet Advanced Training (CAT) which has three programs: serving as a leader during CBT, serving in a field Army unit and attendance at a military school such as Air Assault School. Cadets can also attend Airborne School, Northern Warfare, Combat Diver Qualification Course and the Sapper Leader's Course. Firsties participate in Cadet Troop Leading Training (CTLT) which is a month long troop-leading experience when cadets go to one of 27 plus worldwide Army units and act as platoon leaders, leading real soldiers in the field. As an alternative to CTLT, second class cadets may attend the Drill Cadet Leader Program (DCLT) and act as platoon trainers and company executive officers. DCLT training is held at Fort Benning, GA; Fort Jackson, SC; Fort Sill, OK and Fort Leonard Wood, MO. Upperclass cadets are also required to serve in a variety of leadership positions during one of their last two summers. They can serve as platoon leader to Regimental Commander during CBT or CFT to further develop their leadership skills as they train and lead new cadets or third class cadets.

The Military Science Branch consists of eight Military Science core courses designed as a continuum of summer military training. Military Science core courses are complemented and supplemented by a Warfighters' lecture series, Joint Professional Military Education, tactical decision-making exercises, combat simulations and the faculty sharing their experiences on the battlefield. DMI has high-tech facilities such as the War-fighting Simulation Center which provides an educational laboratory. Here cadets can apply what they've learned in class in Ground Maneuver Warfare and learn using the most current Military Information Technology and Simulation.

The Branching Program introduces cadets to the Army Branches: Air Defense, Armor, Aviation, Chemical, Engineering, Field Artillery, Finance, Infantry, Medical Corps, Military Intelligence, Military Police, Ordnance, Quartermaster, Signal, Transportation and Adjutant General. DMI also offers six Cadet Military Clubs. The West Point Parachute Team, known as the Black Knights, are featured on pages 128 and 129. The Infantry Tactics Club, the Combat Weapons Team, the Calvary and Scout Club, the Pistol Team and the Law Enforcement Tactics Team are clubs that give cadets the opportunity to practice their field skills during the academic year.

The Cadet Leadership Development is a branch of DMI that integrates and organizes cadet leader development experiences, articulates principles, standards, and values, provides goals for developmental programs and offers a framework for progressive leader-subordinate experience. This branch works closely with the Department of Behavioral Science and Leadership and their courses.

The Combating Terrorism Center seeks to provide future and current Army leaders with the tools needed to overcome and discourage terrorist threats to our nation. Founded in February 2003, the Center has been proactive in supporting the Global War on Terror. The Center utilizes the expertise of its staff to provide cadets with the chance to study homeland security, terrorism and counterterrorism.

Finally, the Simon Center for Professional Military Ethic is the Academy's hub for developing professional Officership within the Corps of Cadets. It integrates into cadet life "The 7 Army Values" - Loyalty, Duty, Respect, Selfless Service, Honor, Integrity, Personal Courage and the "Cadet Honor Code: A Cadet will not lie, cheat, steal or tolerate those who do." It is also the sponsor of research, writing and teaching on Professional Military Ethic. Character development is a vital part of cadet training and education and is also pervasive in a cadet's life. The Respect Program Advisory Council teaches cadets to live a life of ethical and moral excellence through mentorship and education. The Honor Committee serves the Corp of Cadets as stewards of the Honor System. These elected volunteers oversee hearings, conduct honor investigations and assist in the U.S. Army Professional Military Ethic. The focus on intense and rigorous summer training and the emphasis on ethics and character development are additional aspects of the West Point experience that distinguish it from civilian colleges.

MEETING OF ENTIRE CLASS TO REVIEW PROCEDURES

In the Robinson Auditorium (Thayer Hall), the **COMMANDANT OF CADETS IS ADDRESSING AN ENTIRE CLASS OF CADETS**. The Commandant commands the Corps of Cadets, oversees the instruction and integration of the Professional Military Ethic and supervises the Physical and Military programs. This is one of numerous meetings that are held throughout the year to review military procedures and decorum. USMA provides 24% of the Army's lieutenants, but graduates make up 34% of the Army's 2, 3 and 4-star Generals. The Commandant is instilling in this class of cadets what they need in today's world to continue the duty given to our country by the Long Gray Line.

CADET ANSWER S TOUGH QUESTIONS FROM ACADEMY MEDIA

MILITARY INSTRUCTION - PUBLIC SPEAKING

CLASS IN WHAT TO SAY TO THE MEDIA

CLASS IN WHAT TO SAY TO THE MEDIA

Shown above is **CLASS INSTRUCTION FOR DMI** in how to appropriately respond to the media in various potentially problematic scenarios. Each cadet's performance is taped and then reviewed. Eight Military Science courses are required with each academic year building on the prior year's instruction leading to an ability to think and communicate militarily. Cadets can major in Military Arts and Sciences. The opportunity to apply what is learned in class during the academic year is given during summer training and is shown in the following pages.

CARRY YOUR FELLOW NEW CADET

HAND TO HAND COMBAT INSTRUCTION

OBSTACLE COURSE SET UP FOR NEW CADETS

GETTING THROUGH THE COURSE

Six week training for new cadets known as **CADET BASIC TRAINING (CBT) ALSO KNOWN AS BEAST BARRACKS**, revolves around demanding physical activities, basic soldier skills, discipline and courtesy. New cadets are pushed to the edge of their limits physically and mentally and participate in events that they probably never dreamed of. Failing and continuing are part of the new lesson to be learned. Training for new cadets includes a Physical Training test, Drill Competition, Bayonet Assault, Individual Tactics, a Leader Reaction Course, Close Quarters Combat, etc. Training used to involve more yelling at cadets but since General John Abizaid was Commandant, the trainers are no longer a part of the problem but a part of the solution.

NEW CADETS OBSTACLE COURSE

MOVING YOUR FELLOW NEW CADETS

OBSTACLE COURSE - GETTING EVERYONE OVER THE WALL

PULL UPS TILL YOU FALL OFF

New cadets will not officially become plebes until they pass the six weeks of **CBT** sometimes referred to by cadets as **BEAST BARRACKS**. Shown above are a couple of the many events requiring teamwork. Teamwork and success are linked hand-in-hand at West Point and most new cadets catch on quickly. The individualistic tendencies that make a student a fit for West Point are also the tendencies that need modification. General George Custer and his men paid the ultimate price due to his ego and arrogance. West Point does its best to make sure that doesn't happen again.

PREPARATION FOR THE HOUSE OF TEARS

HOUSE OF TEARS

PREPARATION FOR THE HOUSE OF TEARS

EXITING THE HOUSE OF TEARS

Part of **CBT-BEAST BARRACKS** includes entering a building filled with tear gas, sometimes lovingly referred to as the "house of tears." New cadets are given instruction before donning the mask and entering the building on what to expect and what not to do. Some cadets learn the hard way not to panic and remove their mask prematurely. CBT is as demanding on the upperclassmen leading as it is on new cadets learning humility and how to follow. It is an extreme learning curve for all involved and new cadets who don't make the grade this summer will not get a spring break.

25 FOOT RAPPEL AND CLIMB

75 FOOT RAPPEL

25 FOOT RAPPEL

CLIMB UP THE 75 FOOT CLIFF

BEAST BARRACKS-CBT also includes an exciting or torturous climb and rappel up a 25″ and then a 75′ rock wall. This training is not optional for anyone and all must pass; even those that might have a fear of heights have to overcome that fear. The Army has to know that when it's officers are put in a potentially frightening situation they will be able to cope and perform no matter what. The responsibility for seeing that new cadets succeed falls squarely on the shoulders of the upperclassmen and the best leaders will inspire cadets to perform and meet new challenges.

TRAINING IN FORCED ENTRY

CONVOY PROTECTION

MILITARY CHECKPOINT

DEMONSTRATION OF "BONECRUSHER" FOR LANDMINES

DMI modifies it's training to fit world situations. The entire battalion-level training 13 day exercise called **OPERATION HIGHLAND WARRIOR** introduces cadets to the Patriot weapon system, 50 caliber machine gun firing and how to properly and thoroughly search civilians or potential threats to the U.S. Army. Cadets shown above are part of a Military Check Point exercise and convoy protection and patrol. Protection of military convoys is becoming a critical issue for military operational planners facing modern guerilla warfare threats and the convoy is accompanied by heavily armored escort vehicles.

CORDON AND SEARCH OPERATIONS

CORDON AND SEARCH OPERATIONS

CORDON AND SEARCH OPERATIONS

ANALYSIS OF CORDON AND SEARCH OPERATIONS

Also part of **OPERATION HIGHLAND WARRIOR** is a cordon and search exercise, a new modification to DMI's training to reflect current world situations. The cadet with the machine gun pulled the "short straw" and gets to haul around an extra 25 pounds in the heat. After training exercises, cadets are debriefed on how well they performed the cordon and search maneuver and where they made errors. Cadets are expected to make mistakes and learn from them, period. When their time at Camp Buckner is over, cadets have a long, hot run back to the post area.

TRAINING DEMONSTRATION OF MOBILE ARTILLERY

TRAINING DEMONSTRATION OF ARMORED ARTILLERY

TRAINING DEMONSTRATION OF MOBILE ROCKET LAUNCHER

HANDS ON TRAINING ON 105MM HOWITZER

Above, cadets are learning about **ARTILLERY SUPPORT** and the mobile artillery weapons used in the field. These weapons are not for long range but are specialized for mobility and tactical efficiency. Soldiers currently employ three main types of Field Artillery weapons systems. The M102 (105mm) shown above cadets learn to fire and is one of three towed howitzer weapon systems in use. The M270 Multiple Launch Rocket System (MLRS) is the Field Artillery's heaviest and longest-ranged weapons system, a self-propelled rocket launcher using 270 mm unguided rockets.

TRAINING DEMONSTRATION OF MOBILE ARTILLERY

The blast from a firing Howitzer can be heard for miles through the Hudson Valley during the summer. It is both awesome to watch and hear. In most **FIELD ARTILLERY** situations, the soldiers using the guns can't see the target they are firing upon because of various obstacles such as mountains and valleys or poor visibility due to weather or nighttime conditions. The gunners have to rely on a trained artillery observer who sees the target and relays the coordinates of the target. These coordinates are translated into a left-right aiming direction, then an elevation angle and the number of bags of propellant needed and last, the waiting time for the lighting of the fuze in order to hit the target.

105

For one week of CFT, yearlings (sophomores) also go to Fort Knox, Kentucky and become acquainted with **ARMOR AND MECHANIZED INFANTRY** equipment and the Army's more heavy forces. What has the firepower of a tank, has state-of-the-art communications technology, goes 60mph and can be transported by the Army within 96 hours to anyplace in the world? The Stryker, pictured above. Cadets being are briefed on the capabilities and fire power of the Stryker, an eight-wheel drive armored combat vehicle.

INSTRUCTION ON THE BRADLEY AND THE M-240 CHAIN MACHINE GUN

INSTRUCTION ON THE M-240 MEDIUM MACHINE GUN

INSTRUCTION ON MK-19 GRENADE MACHINE GUN

COMMANDANT OF CADETS TALKS WITH CADETS

CADETS AT FT KNOX get an inside look at the Bradley Infantry Fighting Vehicle which is used to transport infantry on the battlefield, to provide fire cover to dismounted troops and to suppress enemy tanks and fighting vehicles. Cadets also are given instruction on the M240B medium machine gun on the Humvee and MK-19 grenade machine gun also mounted on a Humvee. Each cadet gets a turn to fire all of the weapons shown above. In the lower right photo, the Commandant is talking with cadets about their Fort Knox experience.

Also known as Mounted Maneuver Training and the Calvary, cadets train in tank simulators as a gunner and a driver, get an **INTRODUCTION TO THE ABRAMS TANK** and it's weapons and eventually get to live fire an Abrams. During CFT, cadets are given a show on how well the Calvary can move these tanks. A "pep" talk follows an awesome demonstration by the Calvary to further fire up cadets about learning to maneuver tanks and fire tank weapons.

THE ABRAMS TANK is shown on both pages and is powered by two gas turbine engines. Cadets wear special fire-retardant gear before firing an Abrams. The sound of an Abrams firing is deafening and vibrates one to the core. Operation Thunder Strike is a mounted "force on force" mock battle with cadet companies engaging each other in Abrams M1A2 tanks. The intent by the Calvary Enlisted and Officers here is to show the maneuverability and awesome power of these tanks in order to recruit as many cadets as possible to the Calvary branch.

109

AIR ASSAULT OBSTACLE COURSE

AIR ASSAULT OBSTACLE COURSE

AIR ASSAULT OBSTACLE COURSE

AIR ASSAULT is just one of 13 training opportunities available to second year cadets, such as Fire Support, Bayonet Assault, Mounted Movement training, etc. Air Assault school takes place year round at various locations but for cadets it is based at Camp Smith for 10 days. The physical fitness prerequisites for enrolling in Air Assault are high. Cadets and enrolled Army enlisted and officers go through intense physical training with practical learning and some classwork. The instructors are very professional and experienced and push everyone beyond their limits. Training starts with the famous (or infamous to some) obstacle course at Camp Buckner followed by a paced five-mile march at the end of the day. Noncompletion of either means "you're out" without getting your "wings."

AIR ASSAULT OBSTACLE COURSE

AIR ASSAULT EQUIPMENT CHECK

AIR ASSAULT RELAXATION AFTER FIVE MILE MARCH

AIR ASSAULT EQUIPMENT CHECK

AIR ASSAULT training is less about training to rappel out of helicopters and more about teaching the basic aspects of air assault operations. There are three phases: Combat Assault, Slingload Operations and Rappelling with a written or applied exam after each phase of training. Failure of either can result in a "no-go." Everyone in Air Assault training is expected to have the necessary gear and have it in order. Inspections are done regularly and rigorous physical activity is almost non-stop. No one is allowed to have alcohol or tobacco and anyone caught with either substance is out, even if it is their last day of training. Long-lasting bonds are formed with peers and those leading instruction during these intense 10 days.

111

REWARD FOR NOT HAVING RAPPEL GEAR CORRECT

RAPPELLING FROM TOWER

RAPPELLING FROM TOWER

CHECKING GEAR BEFORE RAPPEL

AIR ASSAULT Cadets are given instruction on how to secure their rappel gear and have to show the Army personnel in charge of training that they can hook-up, lock-in, etc. before they rappel. The "hip rappel seat" has to be tied in less than 90 seconds and hook-up to a rappel rope in 15 seconds, correctly. Before they drop, they give a shout, wait for the okay, lean back into space, get into position, then jump back. The thrill of rappelling down a high tower high has to be incredible but Air Assault is supposed to end with two rappels with and without combat equipment from a Blackhawk helicopter at 70-90'. During this training session weather kept the Blackhawk from landing.

BLACKHAWK DROPS OFF AIR ASSAULT TRAINEES

The Blackhawk can move a squad of 11 troops in the most adverse situations. **AIR ASSAULT** landing zones are as small as any patch of ground where a chopper can land or anything the pilot can hover above. Cadets learn to communicate with the chopper crew and board and depart from a helicopter under combat conditions (blades spinning) without getting injured or worse. Contrast this training with civilian life where one is instructed never to leave the helicopter until the blades have completely stopped. Cadets are flown around in the Blackhawk several times to get used the movement, fumes, boarding and departing. The last day ends with a timed 12 mile march under full combat load, kevlar and all- then they're awarded their wings.

No other game has greater prestige or deeper roots than the **ARMY/NAVY GAME.** An annual college football game usually played on the last weekend of the regular season in early December, pits the football team of West Point against the United States Naval Academy. It is one of the most traditional and enduring rivalries in college football, and is televised every year. The rivalry started 117 years ago when Cadet Dennis Mahan Michie accepted a challenge offered by the Naval Academy. The first organized game took place on The Plain on November 29 in 1890. A visit to West Point just prior to the annual rivalry will impress the visitor with how deep and enduring this tradition is.

ATHLETICS & PHYSICAL DEVELOPMENT

The Department of Physical Education develops cadets to be physically fit leaders through a challenging Physical Education and Sports Program, "Every cadet an athlete, every athlete challenged." Contrasted with normal civilian college, cadets are expected to be in top physical condition and are required to pass all core physical education courses, physical fitness tests every fall and spring and Indoor Obstacle Course Tests as well as participate in a competitive sport, whether club, intramural or corps squad sports. Cadets, like all military personnel, are expected to, at a minimum, meet optimum standards for appearance, body composition and fitness. The Army Operations Manual states that the "U.S. Army forces must be prepared to fight and win on short notice anywhere in the world, from blistering deserts to frigid wastelands, in rain forests, tundra, mountains, jungles and swamps, urban sprawl and all types of terrain in between," meaning men and women are expected to be ready to perform various duties under conditions that can be incredibly adverse. Cadets are required to display readiness at all times, in Army terms, meaning maximum fitness, health and ability to perform.

The program is integrated with cadet summer training giving cadets an unparalled physical development program not found in civilian universities. Also embedded within the program are a number of Army requirements needed to be commissioned as an Army officer. The department develops a will to win, capacity for team-work, initiative and self-confidence as well as an extensive knowledge of fitness science. The faculty that teaches and coaches within the department lead by example.

Fourth Class or Plebe Physical Education ensures that all cadets obtain a baseline level of physical fitness and motor skills. Third Class Physical Education Program focuses on wellness, physical readiness and self-confidence, with an emphasis on The Combatives that prepares cadets for self-defense situations. The purpose of the Second Class Physical Education Program is to ensure cadets continue to develop optimum levels of physical fitness as well as a thorough understanding of the principles and theories that support a healthy, active lifestyle. During the Second Class year, the Army Physical Fitness Test (APFT) is formally evaluated in the spring and fall. First Class Physical Education Program continues to develop a cadet's physical fitness and movement and focuses on leadership skills. A mandatory course for all Firsties is registration in one Lifetime Sport which is designed to give cadets all that they need to solidify a life-long habit of physical fitness and activity.

Cadets participate in Competitive Club Sports including boxing, crew, cycling, equestrian, fencing, women's lacross, mountaineering, powerlifting, skiing, rugby and more. They also have the opportunity chose from one of 25 different intercollegiate athletic teams ranging from basketball and football to soccer, rugby and boxing. At least 18 of the Academy's 25 teams compete in the Patriot League. The winter months are the busiest with 10 teams competing on an intercollegiate level. During the spring, Army competes in baseball, tennis, lacrosse, golf and outdoor track for men, and softball, tennis and outdoor track for women, all a member of the Patriot League. Rifle is Army's only coed sport. Over 25% of the Corps of Cadets competes on the intercollegiate level.

The Morale, Welfare and Recreation Department has a variety of regular leisure activities for cadets, soldiers, civilian employees and retirees. The West Point Golf Course, Bowling Center, Morgan Farm and Kennel and other special events throughout the year are open to the general public. The Physical Education Department has fitness standards that must be met and kept, and offers an array of competitive opportunities for cadets to develop physical fitness, teamwork, a sense of fair play, dedication and preparation, all of which lead to prepared Army officers.

ARMY NAVY GAME

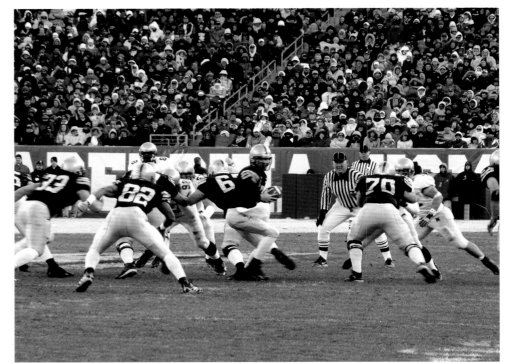

ARMY NAVY GAME

ARMY NAVY GAME

ARMY NAVY GAME

The fun and majesty of **ARMY-NAVY GAMES** games are obvious to any attendee. Devoted fans sit in the cold of early December to watch the drama unfold, usually held in Philadelphia which is about equidistant from both academics. The Army mascot has been the mule since 1899 which reminds one of the usefulness mules had in the past for the Army by transporting guns, ammunition and supplies. The awe of seeing the Corps of Cadets march onto the field in perfect unison and then enthusiastically run to their seats in a massive swell of gray, and the cannon blasts that shake Michie to its core when the Black Knights score, are just part of the splendor of an Army-Navy game.

116

ARMY NAVY GAME

ARMY FOOTBALL AT MICHIE STADIUM

ARMY NAVY GAME

ARMY FOOTBALL AT MICHIE STADIUM

ARMY/NAVY passion is evident even in the history of the 10 times that the game was not played. Only a few years after the football rivalry began, an incident between a Brigadier General and a Rear Admiral almost led to a duel after Navy's victory. The intense rivalry was defused for five years after President Cleveland called a Cabinet meeting and the two teams were "prohibited in engaging in games elsewhere." In other words, the two teams were kept from playing each other and for the next five years, the explosive rivalry was defused. The excitement of **ARMY FOOTBALL** generates a huge following and sellout crowds are customary at Michie Stadium.

117

ARMY CREW is one of our favorite teams- cadets pay $500 to purchase their boat and are top-notch in their sport and the team's success is based on both individual performance as well as the sum of its parts. The crew coach and team constantly assess team dynamics and what makes a winning team.   Since it's beginning in 1986, the team has been competing on the East Coast and competes in 3-5 national races annually. During the spring the team competes every weekend from the beginning of April through the second week of May. After the fall season, the crew works out hard during the winter and ends with a week-long training session during spring break.

The **ARMY SWIMMING AND DIVING TEAM** trains rigorously six days a week and works hard year-round to prepare for its peak performance against Navy and the Patriots. Army's Crandall pool is considered one of the best venues on the East Coast and the team takes full advantage of the West Point facilities. **ARMY HOCKEY** became a member of the Metro Atlantic Athletic Conference Hockey League in 2000. Army regularly clinches home ice in fast action at Tate Rink which is one of the most popular rinks on the East Coast because its seating arrangement offers fans a cozy seat close to the action.

ARMY TRACK AND FIELD is one of the most physically and mentally demanding sports that doesn't always get the attention it deserves. Above are javelin, pole vaulting and track at Shea Stadium, one of the finest facilities in the East, with six long jump/triple jump runways, four pole vault runways, two shot-put areas and two Olympic discus/hammer throw sectors. A state-of-the-art timing system allows cadets to run in either direction with a photo finish. Army's indoor track and field facility is inside of Gillis Field house. Qualifying times in straight races, throws and jumps are more easily reached at West Point than most other indoor facilities, making West Point appealing to the best in the sport.

MEN'S ARMY SOCCER TEAM

ARMY WRESTLING

WOMEN'S ARMY SOCCER TEAM

WOMEN'S ARMY VOLLEYBALL

Clinton Field is home to men's and women's **ARMY SOCCER**. Both teams are top in their sport and enjoy the Soccer Clubhouse, across from Clinton which has locker room facilities, a training area and meeting room and lounge for the team. **ARMY WRESTLING** practices at new facilities in Arvin. Every week after winter break, Army sends out 10 dedicated cadets to represent West Point on wrestling mats throughout the country and they do it well. The dedicated women cadets in **ARMY VOLLEYBALL** give fans a fast-paced and exciting game. The team earned recognition from the NCAA for its Academic Progress Rate scores.

AEROBICS CLASSES

SKIING

WEIGHT TRAINING

SKIING

AEROBICS classes are offered to cadets in the Arvin Cadet Physical Development Center. West Point has one of the world's best physical development programs. **WEIGHT TRAINING** is available to all cadets at Arvin, a 495,000 square foot gym facility. West Point also has a Powerlifting club sport team that has been competing since 1982. **SKIING** is available at West Point to all cadets, competitive and non-competitive and for all levels of skiers. The slopes are well maintained and groomed and a fun way to spend a winter Sunday.

Another outstanding facility available to cadets is the 48-foot high **ROCK-CLIMBING** wall in Arvin, donated by the class of 1979. West Point has some nice outdoor climbing facilities and the new indoor facility will address the fitness needs for cadets regardless of the weather. Plebes must take a course that begins with lessons on the indoor climbing wall. The Cadet Mountaineering Club practices here when they're not climbing the cliffs along the Hudson and climbs various places around the country. The club practices daily and try-outs begin in the fall of each year and are based on a good standing in the corps, prior climbing ability as well as try-out performance. The new indoor wall is a much friendlier place to practice during the winter months.

BOXING TEAM

BRIGADE SPIRIT TEAM PRACTICE

BOXING TEAM

BRIGADE SPIRIT TEAM PRACTICE

The **BOXING TEAM** offers cadets an opportunity to compete at the highest level possible and the team is more nationally competitive each year with Bronze, Silver and Gold Medalists. The facilities in Arvin where they practice is enormous and the best available. The 26 member **BRIGADE SPIRIT TEAM** is a group of superb athletes. Cheerleading is not usually thought of as a sport, but is physically very demanding and requires many skills. It is recommended that anyone wanting to be a cheerleader for the Black Knights have a background in gymnastics, which after watching their amazing flips and tumbles, one can understand why gymnastics skills are necessary.

124

WOMEN'S TENNIS TEAM

GYMNASTICS TEAM

WOMEN'S TENNIS TEAM

GYMNASTICS TEAM

The **WOMEN'S TENNIS** team is shown practicing in the Lichtenberg Tennis Center. The center has had a positive impact on the performance of both men and women's tennis with it's seven-court arena with state-of-the-art lighting, a sophisticated synthetic indoor hard-court surface and elevated spectator area that gives avid fans a great view of all of the courts. The **GYMNASTICS TEAM** regularly finishes in the top of its competitions and also has outstanding facilities where they can hone their skills to compete with the best around the country.

The **WOMEN'S BASKETBALL** team shown above won the NCAA Division I Tournament for the 2005-06 season. The team plays at Christl Arena located in Holleder which is an excellent facility for the Black Knights men's and women's basketball. The arena has a Horner hardwood floor, fixed chair and bench seating that offers a great view from all angles. It hosts up to 5,043 avid basketball fans.

Army's **BASEBALL TEAM** gives fans exciting games. If you look closely at the picture above, you can see the ball as it heads toward 3rd base. The team recently had two of its players chosen this year for the top 10 round of Major League Baseball's First-Year Player Draft. They play at Doubleday Field, named after Abner Doubleday, a West Point grad (1842) who is rumored to have developed the game of baseball. He called the game "Base Ball" similar to a game called "rounders" played in England. As a Captain, Doubleday fired the first gun for the Union side of the Civil War at Fort Sumter.

The **WEST POINT PARACHUTE TEAM-THE BLACK KNIGHTS** is actually a Department of Military Instruction Club. They have the honor of using the Superintendent's helicopter for their jumps. The team competes at the national and collegiate level and jumps the game ball into Michie Stadium each year for every Army home football game and perform at other venues around the country. The team is capable of jumping into any open field and the main reason for their performances is to leave a positive impression of West Point on the audience. The cadets remain available to answer any questions the audience may have after a demonstration.

The **WEST POINT PARACHUTE TEAM-THE BLACK KNIGHTS** is capable of utilizing flags, smoke or streamers in their demonstrations to add to the drama and complexity of a performance. They are awesome to watch and the excitement of a jump is captured in the photo above as a team member is captured floating in the sky with the moon behind them. Any member of the team who jumps for a public performance must have met the jump requirements for a special license that is given by the FAA. The highlight of their year is the Collegiate National Skydiving Competition where they have the opportunity to challenge a number of colleges, including the Air Force Academy in two-way and four-way formation skydiving. They frequently walk away with almost half of the 75 medals.

The cadets move in perfect unison, as one. Marching is a sometimes grueling part of cadet life. It is not easy to wear a tarbucket and Full Dress in the sun and heat. For four years the graduating class has been waiting for this day. It always seemed far away and finally, the day has arrived. It also marks the beginning of a new year and new responsibilities and privileges for all cadets. **GRADUATION WEEK** is celebrated with the Alumni Review and Distinguished Graduate Award, the Cadet Drill Team Performance, the Superintendent's Awards Review and the Graduation Parade, Graduation Dinner and Hop attended by the graduating First Class and their guests.

GRADUATION WEEK

During graduation week, First Class cadets have a feeling of regret at leaving friends and West Point and yet they are floating on elation as they look toward a new career as Army Officers. Full rehearsal for the Graduation Parade begins early in the week with the Chain of Command practicing and then going back to barracks as the rest of the Corps marches onto the Plain. The First Class wear their class uniform, sabers, white gloves, and dress hat, the tarbucket. They mill around in front of the bleachers while waiting for the rest of the Corps to assemble onto the Plain. The underclassmen look the same as the First Class except they carry rifles instead of sabers. Three thousand strong, they march out to the final line and under the command of the new Second Class, they salute with their rifles, come to attention, to parade rest, present arms and back again. They practice the entire parade until they have it right. The First Class wants their Graduation Parade to be perfect for their proud family and friends and as you can see on page 130 on the Friday before graduation, it truly is a perfect day and a perfect Graduation Parade.

The six days of celebration precede the most anticipated ceremony of all, graduation and commissioning. Graduation Week consists of receptions, parades, Superintendent's Reception, Cadet Parachute demo, drills, dinners, dances and many other festivities. Families, friends and the general public are invited to witness many of the traditional ceremonies. One of the most interesting aspects of military celebrations is that everyone is on time. Civilians don't comprehend that when the Superintendent sends 500 invitations to a reception at 1300 hours, everyone is there a few minutes early and only one person knocks on the door. Three companies at a time show up at the Superintendent's Reception with their families at the assigned time and it takes hours on two days for the Superintendent and his wife to greet each guest in the receiving line.

Graduation Week passes very quickly and on the morning of graduation, family and friends gather at Michie Stadium early. An emotional but exhilarating day, graduation is the climax of 47 indelible, rewarding and often stressful months. The tone is solemn and the ceremony impressive. Among the honorable main speakers are the Superintendent, Commandant, Academic Dean, Secretary of the Army, Army Chief of staff and some years the President or Vice President. After the VIPs give their speeches, it is time to award the diplomas. Combined choirs stand to sing "The Corps" and cadets and past graduates join in the song about the Long Gray Line. The Dean announces that these cadets are receiving their degree of Bachelor of Science and in order of merit, the cadets go to the stage to receive their diplomas. After the honor grads, First Captain and Class President receive their diplomas, two readers and presenters stand at the top of the two ramps leading to the stage and read the cadets' names accurately and quickly. Every time a name is read, there is cheering from the crowd. The loudest cheer of all comes when the name of the class "Goat" is read, the person who academically is at the bottom of the list of grads. The tradition of the Goat is a long one at West Point and includes notable grads as Pickett and Custer. After they are awarded their diplomas, many are over-whelmed and leap into the air, hug each other, drop to their knees, hands clasped, tears in their eyes at the achievement of this momentous moment.

After the last cadet receives his diploma and Bachelor of Science degree, the Alma Mater is sung with passion by all who can sing it, and the Commandant asks the graduating class to raise their right hands, caps removed and solemnly swear to uphold the Constitution of the United States- the Oath of Office. The Superintendent gives the approval to the First Captain who shouts "Class dismissed," and the graduates toss their white hats high into the air, triumphantly. At this point, youngsters in the audience under age 12 are allowed to run out onto the field and retrieve the hats. Cadets will serve 5 years in the military and eligibility for particular branches such as armor, artillery, aviation, infantry, etc. is determined by the cadet's personal preference, academic performance and availability. Cadets can also "cross-commission" and request a commission in the Air Force, Navy or Marine Corps if they meet that service's eligibility requirements. The First Class enters Michie Stadium as cadets and leave as 2nd lieutenants in the Army. They are about to exchange their "grays for green" and assume positions of responsibility as Army officers carrying out the oath of "Duty, Honor, Country."

Much of cadet life revolves around marching, and just when they are about to graduate, the First Class has even more marching the week of graduation. The **CORPS OF CADETS** is made up of teens and those a few years older and yet to the amazement of many civilians (and many parents), these cadets march in perfect form, with perfect uniforms. The Color Guard carries the "Colors" of West Point, the Army and the United States. Military organizations have always carried distinctive symbols which started out as banners. Later flags with distinctive colors and emblems were designed to represent different regiments, known as Colors. In battle, Colors were used as a symbol of spirit and rally point as well as a means of controlling the unit.

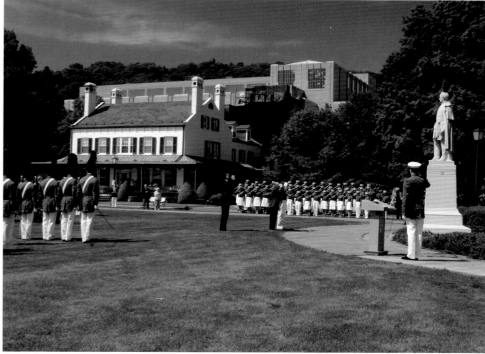

Pictured above is the **ALUMNI REVIEW** and **DISTINGUISHED GRADUATE AWARD.** West Point graduates from 50 to 70 years ago attend the ceremony. On this day, the Long Gray Line is represented by the young cadets and the old veterans. The Distinguished Graduates Award is given to West Point graduates who have supported West Point throughout their lives and have distinguished themselves with their service, character and living West Point's motto, "Duty, Honor, Country." In the lower left picture, the Cadet First Captain is shown assisting the oldest living West Point graduate, a Brigadier General from the class of '32 in placing a wreath honoring Sylvanus Thayer. The bottom picture portrays the new Long Gray Line.

GRADUATION DINNER is a joyous time of celebration with family for First Class cadets who will graduate in the morning at Michie Stadium.   It is a formal event with cadets in Full Dress and civilians in suits, tuxedos and formal long or short dresses.   Everyone is served a home-style meal in amazingly quick order on nicely set tables in Washington Hall.   A memorable night for cadets and their families, all anxiously await the next day.

The **GRADUATION HOP** is held after formal Graduation Dinner on Friday evening in a festively decorated hall. The mood is one of elation as cadets and visitors dance, eat, drink and socialize. Memories are captured here as families and friends pose proudly in the ring with their graduating cadet. The West Point Alma Mater, was first played at the 1909 Graduation Hop. The words were written by then Cadet Reinecke in 1909 who was suddenly inspired one day in the fall while walking about the Area.

It is an emotional time and joyful time before graduation as cadets greet each other, their TAC officers and enlisted, and the Goat outside the stadium. The Goat is the last in the class academically. Jefferson Davis, George Custer, George Pickett and others were "Goats" but made military history. James Whistler and Edgar Allan Poe couldn't make it long enough to become Goats. Whistler was sent home in his third year and Poe was sent home in his first year but both became famous. In 1978, the Academy started listing graduates in alphabetical order, thereby eliminating the name of the Goat. But at graduation, every cadet knows who the Goat is and cheers wildly when the name is called.

Once in the stadium, everyone waits anxiously for the **GRADUATION CEREMONIES** to begin, It has taken four long and short years to get here and the cadets look polished but pensive.   A crowd of thousands of family and friends are seated in Michie about to witness the passage of almost 1,000 First Class cadets to 2nd lieutenants in the Army. After they graduate, their first assignment as an officer is at the Officer Basic Course within their particular branch. Once they complete this course, they will be on their way to leading and training a platoon of soldiers with "Loyalty, Duty, Respect, Selfless Service, Honor, Integrity, Personal Courage."

On the field during **GRADUATION DAY**, the USMA band, Glee Club and Cadet Choir sit on the lower bleachers. Onstage is the Superintendent, Commandant of Cadets, Dean, the Secretary of the Army, other VIPs and every four years, the President of the United States. Behind the graduating class are the TAC officers and NCOs. In the first rows of cadets are the honor graduates and they are the first to accept their diplomas. After the diplomas are awarded, the Corps of Cadets joins older grads in singing the Alma Mater. After the Alma Mater is sung, the Oath of Office is administered by the Commandant. In just minutes these young people have ended one chapter and begun another with the solemn Oath of Office.

The new 2nd lieutenants send their **WHITE HATS SOARING** into the air symbolic of the end of cadet life and the start of a new journey as they trade white cadet caps for the officer's hat. Hats often have notes in them or pictures or even money and children are permitted to go onto the field to retrieve the prize. The ceremonial hat-toss dates to 1946 and it should be noted that cadets are not the only ones graduating at West Point. West Point instructors are both teachers and learners and the rotating military instructors who are about to return to the field as field-grade officers are better able to meet the challenges they will face because of their training as instructors.

After the ceremonial hat-toss, cadets hug each other, their TAC officers, family and family grads of West Point. This is an emotional time for all and a celebration of incredible achievement. They started out as high-achieving and physically fit high-school teens and are now disciplined, ethical, knowledgeable and well-trained Army officers. In creating this book, we were struck by the fact that close to 75% of these "kids" and Officers were about embark on a mission that made us proud of them and saddened us at the same time.

Seen above are proud family and friends with their new 2nd Lieutenants, hugging, taking pictures and celebrating their cadet and now Officer's accomplishments. For some this is a family tradition, and a prior West Point grad, an Army officer, salutes the new officer and pins on his "butter" bars at Trophy Point. It is also a moment of quiet reflection for some newly commissioned officers to stand on West Point's hallowed grounds and reflect on the years past and the years to come.

Cadets aren't permitted to marry until after they've become commissioned officers. **WEDDINGS** have to be booked months in advance of graduation so that the couple can wed in the majestic Cadet Chapel. If the bride is in the military, she has a choice of marrying in her full dress military uniform or a wedding gown. Most choose a traditional wedding gown but if she decides to wear her military uniform, she still walks down the aisle with a bridal bouquet. The bride stands to the right of the groom if the groom is military because that is the side where his sword is worn.

This elegant and joyful couple have just finished taking their vows inside the Cadet Chapel. The arch of swords is a beautiful tradition that sets **MILITARY WEDDINGS** apart from the civilian ceremony. As soon as the service concludes, the groom's ushers quietly hurry to the outside to stand waiting with their swords blades up. After they've wed, the bride and groom kiss and then pass under the arch of swords. The tradition is meant to ensure the newlywed couple's happy and safe passage through life together.

Every year a **NEW CLASS OF GRADUATES** line up to take their position in the "Long Gray Line." One thing we can all count on is that what they will face will challenge them as much as the graduates who went before them. It will be their fate to rise to the moment when they are called upon to defend our country. What we can take comfort in is that they have beeen trained and conditioned to handle these new challenges better than anyone before them. We can take heart that the West Point experience has prepared them well for the world they will face. Some of the graduates will exceed all expectations and will join the ranks of Notable Graduates.

NOTABLE GRADUATES

During the many times I was privileged to walk the beautiful grounds of West Point and paused at the monuments that pay homage to past graduates, the thought of the Long Gray Line who had also walked there struck me. Distinguished people whom I had known of during my life came to mind: President Dwight D. Eisenhower, General Douglas MacArthur, General George S. Patton, General H. Norman Schwarzkopf, not to mention those that we are honored to have written for this chapter: Astronaut Buzz Aldrin, General Wayne A. Downing, Brigadier General Rebecca Halstead and General Barry McCaffrey. Indeed, the history they teach at West Point was made by those they taught. This chapter page was written with the deepest respect and gratitude. The list of notable grads from West Point and their accomplishments span centuries and the legacy of these graduates are eternally entwined with our nation's history.

In order to appreciate the contributions, character, number and influence of West Point's sons and daughters, one has to consider its beginnings and its circumstances over time. The first graduating class numbered 2 and for years West Point's ranks were small. It took 10 years from its inception in 1802 to reach 70 graduates, and when Robert E. Lee graduated in 1829, the number had grown to 500. But within 11 years, the Long Gray Line swelled 2-fold; by 1840, when General William Sherman graduated, there were more than 1,000 who had graduated from West Point. It took another century for that number to reach 10,000 and after 200 years in 2002, West Point graduates numbered more than 60,000.

The future of West Point graduates and history of our country lies not just in their education, training, character and abilities, but also with politics and fate. Sylvanus Thayer was the only graduate of the 15 in his class of 1808 to achieve the rank of General. He was sent to study the European schools, particularly the French L'Ecole Polytechnique and in 1817, as Superintendent and under his guiding hand, West Point established itself as the nation's finest school of engineering and science. West Point graduates held key positions in nearly every facet of American life and decades before the Civil War began in 1861, grads served as teachers, writers and practitioners of science and engineering at many colleges, including Yale, Harvard and Cornell. West Point grads also began to fill the Army's ranks as junior officers, many later rising to command both the Union and Confederate armies during the Civil War, brother against brother.

More than 75% of West Point graduates fought in the Civil War led by notable graduates such as Stonewall Jackson, P.G.T.Beauregard, Phillip Sheridan, William Tecumseh Sherman, George Armstrong Custer and of course the immortals, Confederate General Robert Robert E. Lee and the leading Union General who later became president, Ulysses S. Grant. After the war ended, the remaining living graduates reconciled more quickly than the rest of our nation and in 1869, graduates from the north and south gathered to form the Association of Graduates. From the late 1860s until the 1890s, the United States maintained only a small army of 25,000, its officers mostly West Point graduates. With no potential for war on the horizon, the army's duties were oriented to completing the conquest of the American Indians.

As the new century began, West Point was evolving and its evolution was accelerated by conflicts in Europe. The fifty years following the Civil War, life in America was completely rearranged as we changed from being a mostly agrarian society to an increasingly urban and industrial one. It was West Point graduates that oversaw the construction of the Washington Monument dedicated in 1885, the tallest masonry structure in the world, the Library of Congress in 1897 and one of the greatest and most difficult engineering undertakings, the construction of the Panama Canal completed in 1914. During the latter part of the 1800's, the Army became progressively more technically adept, career-oriented and apolitical. West Point graduates advanced sophisticated schools for the training of officers. The Spanish-American War in 1898 led to a larger regular army. West Point graduates led the establishment of the War Department General Staff, the Army War College and the organization of the National Guard. By the time the United States entered World War I, our armed forces had increased greatly but by European standards, was still fairly small. West Point graduates led almost every major staff bureau and field command.

In World War I, the scope of mobilization expanded beyond all previous experience. Producing and distributing the vast amounts of supplies, equipment, and munitions required by armies of millions across Europe became a focus of West Point graduates. Trench warfare, more siege than battle, marked the triumph of the engineers and artillerists. It was a kind of war for which West Point training seemed especially apt. The American Expeditionary Force would break this deadlock imposed by mechanized firepower as soon as General John Joseph Pershing (Class of 1886) built an independent American army. Large-scale American combat began 1918 and accelerated the final exhaustion of German reserves and the Armistice on November 11 that ended the war.

World War I mobilization seriously disrupted West Point. General Douglas MacArthur (Class of 1903) was appointed Superintendent after WWI and took action to prepare West Point for her new role and oversaw the Academy's restoration to peak condition. Recalled to active duty in World War II, he led American and Allied Forces in the Pacific to victory over Japan and ended his career as commander of United Nations forces in the Korean War.

Although World War II was not as disruptive, it stimulated even more far-reaching reforms and produced a lot of Generals. The West Point class of 1915 "The Class the Stars Fell On," numbered 164. Over one third of that extraordinary class won stars. The two who attained the army's highest possible rank were Dwight David Eisenhower and Omar Nelson Bradley. Before World War II only four men had held that rank: Ulysses S. Grant (Class of 1843), William T. Sherman (1840), Philip H. Sheridan (1853), and John J. Pershing (1886). Two other West Point graduates attained the rank during World War II, Douglas MacArthur (1903) and Henry H. Arnold (1907). There have been no others to this date.

Major General Davidson (1922) returned to West Point in 1956 as Superintendent; he firmly believed that a changing world demanded major changes at West Point. He was the most successful academic reformer since Sylvanus Thayer and is known for introducing electives, breathing life into the Honor Code and making athletic participation a requirement. Largely unknown outside the army, General Creighton Williams Abrams rose through increasingly responsible positions to four-star rank. His greatest challenge came when he took command of American forces in Vietnam in 1968. The army Abrams (M1) battle tank is named for him.

For America, the Army and for West Point, Vietnam was disheartening. West Point recovered and added new highly decorated heroes to the Long Gray Line. These leaders were victorious in subsequent conflicts such as the triumphant defeat in the Gulf and Operation Desert Storm and numerous have served with honor in Iraq. Many notable grads have gone on to distinguish themselves in a variety of areas like sports, the private sector, industry, national and international politics and astronautics. West Point graduates helped staff the Naval Academy and the Air Force Academy. It should be remembered that all soldiers fighting for democracy are notable. The four notable graduates in the pages that follow who share with us their thoughts on West Point are eminent examples of the Long Gray Line. Though the institution and campus have evolved in many ways over the last 205 years, the Oath of Office, dedication and selfless service given by West Point graduates has not and this historical fortress is a testimony that "Old Soldiers Never Die."

GENERAL WAYNE A. DOWNING, CLASS OF 1962

I grew up with a deep respect for the military and especially the Army. I think this was rooted in my experiences as a small boy during WW II. All the male members of my family served in the armed forces. In fact, the only man I remember being home during this period was my Grandfather. Soldiers received special treatment from our family. I can remember my Grandfather picking up hitchhiking soldiers and going 100 miles out of his way to drop them off at a farm or bringing them home for a meal. At the end of the war, all returned except my father who had been KIA in Germany in March, 1945.

As a young man I read all the military history I could get my hands on, and decided at an early age to try for West Point. In high school I applied for a competitive appointment as the son of a deceased war veteran and gained admission as a member of the Class of 1962.

West Point in the late 1950s was not a kind and gentle place. This naïve kid from central Illinois was in for a real shock. I remember during the first day that I thought a lot of the shenanigans of our Beast Barracks detail were funny to the point of being ludicrous and I laughed. Big mistake, I was singled out for special attention for the next few weeks.

The first year was miserable and basically intolerable, had it not been for my classmates. We all learned early in the game that surviving at West Point was not an individual achievement but would take the concerted effort of all of us working together to hold the upper classmen at bay. We coped with and eventually defeated the oppressive and soulless "system." I learned teamwork, sacrifice, and tolerance to a degree I never thought possible.

I encountered Officer role models in both the Tactical and the Academic Departments as well as fellow Cadets that inspired and developed me. The officers were WW II or Korean War veterans. I later served with some of them and they became life-long friends. The military life style at West Point appealed to me and I grew in confidence, knowledge, and ability.

Just three weeks before our graduation, the Corps of Cadets received a rare visit from one of the Academy's most distinguished graduates: General Douglas MacArthur delivered his famous Farewell Address to the Corps on May 12, 1962 in Washington Hall following noon meal.

I can still hear his soft, hoarse, emotional words that were so prophetic and were to govern the rest of our lives.

"'Duty,' 'Honor,' 'Country' - those three hallowed words reverently dictate what you want to be, what you can be, what you will be. They are your rallying point to build courage when courage seems to fail, to regain faith when there seems to be little cause for faith, to create hope when hope becomes forlorn. … They build your basic character. They mold you for your future roles as the custodians of the nation's defense. They make you strong enough to know when you are weak, and brave enough to face yourself when you are afraid."

My class, 600 strong, went on to face the challenges of our generation guided by the words MacArthur described. We served in the Cold War, did multiple tours in Vietnam, fought the nation's small wars in the shadows, and triumphed in the deserts of the Arabian peninsula. We also became leaders in the private and public sectors as educators, financiers, businessmen, doctors, and ministers. From our ranks came a Medal of Honor recipient (Lieutenant Frank Reasoner, USMC), almost 400 career officers, twenty six general officers, at least two billionaires, two score or more millionaires, numerous company presidents and vice presidents, and a Federal judge.

I am proud of my classmates and the unique Academy that spawned us. Our bonds have become stronger with the passing of the years as we realize how important West Point was in our development and how vital each of us was to the other. Attending West Point was the watershed experience of my life. It set me on course to lead a productive and rewarding life in service to my God, my country, the Army, and my family.

GENERAL WAYNE A. DOWNING *is a highly decorated veteran who has served in diverse command assignments culminating with his appointment as Commander-in-Chief of the U.S. Special Operations Command. Recognized as a top authority on terrorism, he has served in numerous positions, including membership on the National Commission on Terrorism, more recently as the National Director and Deputy National Security Advisor for Combating Terrorism and several private-sector boards.*

GENERAL BARRY McCAFFREY, CLASS OF 1964

In July 1960 I reported in as a New Cadet at the age of 17 straight from my Senior Year at Phillips Andover. I can still remember the incredible excitement as the Class of 1964 was sworn into the Army out on Trophy Point— and a sense that I was coming home. My Dad, Bill McCaffrey, was Class of 1939 and a highly decorated infantry combat veteran of the fighting in the Italian Theater in WWII and the bitter fighting from Inchon to the Yalu in the Korean War. He was a huge influence and example to me growing up. We lived up at Lusk Reservoir at the Academy and I attended 6th through 8th grade years at the West Point Elementary School. Both my uncles were classmates of my Dad…both were also WWII Battle of The Bulge combatants.

I'm almost embarrassed to admit it…but I loved a lot about my four years at West Point including the parades! In particular, I remember the enduring influence and friendships with my classmates – as well as intramural athletics (boxing and soccer), the brilliant instructors in the Department of Social Sciences, and the summer military training. My boxing coach was Frank Reasoner Class of 1962, who had been an All Marine Corps boxer. He was such a hero to all of us. Frank went on to command a Marine Force Recon Platoon in Vietnam where he was killed-in-action and was awarded the Congressional Medal of Honor. To this day I can also remember the thrill of squad combat training during the Plebe encampment as well as the escape from Beast Barracks. The high point of the four years to me was service with an Armored Infantry Battalion in Germany. We deployed by train to Grafenwoer Training Area from our Home Station at Neu Ulm —and I served as a rifle platoon leader in the field for three weeks under the tutelage of a very tough infantry Platoon Sergeant who was a Korean War decorated combat vet.

The Captains and Majors who were our academic instructors and TACs were almost all Korean War combat veterans. Many were in the class of 1950 that had suffered such atrocious losses in the first year of the war. Several were national heroes with incredible combat records described in the military history books we studied. I was impressed by their teaching skills and bright intellects— but I was fascinated by their example and the serious focus they brought to our profession. Many of these wonderful officers went on to be the senior leaders of the Army during the following thirty-two years that I was privileged to serve in uniform. Their friendship and mentoring were a profound influence on me throughout my career.

Looking back on it all from the distance of 42 years since graduation makes me feel a deep sense of gratitude for the formative experience of West Point. My wife Jill and I met and fell in love at West Point. She has been part of the Army with me during the endless moves, three beautiful children and endless separations that followed. There have been some great adventures along the trail of my life as a soldier—as well as some really hard experiences of bloodshed and the loss of fellow soldiers. The boys of '64 whose friendship I so appreciated as a teenager beginning in 1960— went on to be examples of "Duty, Honor, Country" in the decades of peace and war that followed. They look even finer to me now as models of courage and dedication.

West Point was the beginning—but more importantly the Cadet experience was a permanent and continuing presence in our lives through the deeply held values that the four years imprinted on all of us.

GENERAL BARRY R. McCAFFREY was the most highly decorated four-star General in the army upon retirement (DSC plus OLC, Silver Star plus OLC, Purple Heart plus two OLC.) He commanded the 24th Infantry during Desert Storm, served 1996-2001 as the Cabinet Officer for National Drug Policy, and was the Bradley Professor of National Security Studies at West Point from 2001-2005. He is currently President of his own consulting firm and NBC's national security analyst.

BRIGADIER GENERAL REBECCA STEVENS HALSTEAD, CLASS OF 1981

West Point and the Army have been my life since 1977 and if I had the opportunity to do it all over again, I would not change a thing. As a young girl leaving the security of a wonderful home and small town environment from upstate New York, I really had no idea what the future held for me. Unlike so many others who attend the academy, I had no exposure to the military and no specific dreams of growing up to be anything or anyone in particular. However, I did have a strong foundation of patriotism, faith, strong work ethic, humor and discipline. Little did I know then that West Point and the Army were going to be the perfect fit for this country girl.

West Point was an experience for my family and friends, as well. From tailgate parties to Army/Navy games, to Camp Buckner and cheering us on as we finished up Recondo with the slide for life, to being baptized at Delafield Pond, my family and friends participated right along with me. West Point was not just a college experience, it was a life experience. West Point opened the world to me in so many unique and wonderful ways, like traveling overseas to Germany for CTLT and spending one summer break in Greece with my roommate's family (Dena Caradimitropoulo).

As a cadet, the discipline and training prepared me academically, tactically and emotionally to be an Army officer. I was commissioned Ordnance and my first assignment was as a platoon leader (special weapons) in Italy during the Cold War. As the years unfolded, there is no doubt the principles instilled at West Point of discipline, duty, honor and country deepened my character and commitment to service. From battalion command in the 25th Infantry Division (Light) in the Pacific, to brigade command in the 10th Mountain Infantry Division (Light) in New York with service in Afghanistan, to Southern Command (South America) where I had the privilege of serving as the Executive Assistant to the Combatant Commander and learning leadership at the strategic level, to Europe and Iraq as a Commanding General, to my current responsibility as the Army's Chief of Ordnance, these principles shaped my life and influenced my journey.

West Point opened my eyes and heart to the importance of relationships and maintaining them, and has remained a powerful common denominator long after we threw our hats up in the air! Whenever two West Pointers meet there is an instant connection, regardless of "class of" or number of years served. We have shared experiences, emotions and friendships. We have walked those hallowed grounds, felt the sweat drip down our back and the chills run up our necks while standing in Full Dress Gray on the Plain as Old Glory was raised and lowered, listened to the distant train as we laid on our bunks and wished we were on that train no matter where it was headed, and looked out over Trophy Point and dreamed of home, family and friends. The sights and sounds of West Point are forever etched in my memory.

I am certainly proud to be a member of the Class of 1981, "Strength As One, 81!" Our motto then and now reflects the winning power of our combined talents and diversity. Just a few months ago about 12 of us assembled in Baghdad and took a photo in Saddam Hussein's palace. Who would have ever guessed those young adult kids who showed up in July 1977 would become senior leaders in our Army, serve in Iraq and carry the torch for freedom. Our motto reflects life, relationships, families, organizations, our Army, and our Nation! We understood the "12th man" concept when we were cadets and we still do! We surely did not recognize when we were cadets that the events we experienced, the "poop" we memorized, and the relationships we developed on the Hudson would be so instrumental to where we are today and who we have become in our life journeys.

West Point is a military icon but most importantly, it is an American icon. It is where my military journey began, and where my life was shaped mentally, physically, emotionally and spiritually. The academy shaped my profession as an Army officer and led to opportunities I never dreamt possible. As a result, I believe I am a better person and a better American for having had the honor to serve my Nation as part of the Long Gray Line! I would encourage any young adult desiring to find their true potential and use their talents for the greater good of others, to consider attending West Point and serving our Nation.

BRIGADIER GENERAL REBECCA S. HALSTEAD is West Point's first female graduate to become a General. She has received several awards for her meritorious service and was Commanding General of the 3rd Corps Support Command in Iraq until 2006, when she was assigned her present position as Commanding General of the U.S. Army Ordnance Center and Schools in Aberdeen, Maryland.

ASTRONAUT BUZZ ALDRIN, CLASS OF 1951

"Beautiful, beautiful, magnificent desolation." These are the words I spoke the moment I stepped onto the moon and fulfilled a dream with the Eagle and her crew. My journey toward that unforgettable step began the day I was born and West Point was a major impetus toward that historic step. My father favored the Naval Academy as my destiny, but I had other ideas: I wanted to go to West Point and more than anything, I wanted to fly. I came from a military background as my mother was the daughter of a military chaplain and my father served in WWII. He was an aviator in the Army Reserve when I was born and when I was just over two, took me on my first flight in a plane painted to look like an Eagle, all of which furthered the fascination I already had with outer space and the moon. I became particularly enamored when my aunt came home from college with a West Point cadet who had been featured on the cover of Life Magazine. I was in awe of him and knew West Point was for me. I got to know all of the aviators in the Army Air Corps as I grew up, and graduated from high school at age 17 with an outstanding math and science background. In spite of my father trying to steer me toward the Naval Academy, I chose West Point and after four years of excelling in academics and athletics, graduated 3rd in my class with Honors in 1951.

After graduation, my interest in flying was solidified and I was commissioned in the Air Force and started flight training. The timing was such that I was assigned to Korea to fly fighter jets and flew 66 combat missions during the Korean War. West Point creates officers of honor and one experience in particular demonstrates the honesty and courage of West Point Officers. Shortly after I arrived in Korea, I was assigned to the 16th Squadron. We weren't checked out as combat-ready yet and in January of 1953, our Squadron Commander was shot down north of the Yalu River between Korea and Manchuria in a restricted area where we were not supposed to be flying. They grounded us and interviewed different people in the squad about where they were and what had happened when the Commander was shot down. One squad member they interviewed was a West Point officer from the class of '49. He was reprimanded and his career hampered because he told the truth about where they had been flying when the commander was shot down. It is unfortunate that he was punished for his valor and honesty.

After the Korean War, I went on to get a Sc.D. from MIT in 1963 where I wrote my thesis on manned orbital rendezvous. The discipline and strong engineering background I received at West Point served me well at MIT and NASA. I flew on the Gemini 12 space mission in November, 1966 and then was chosen as the lunar module pilot for Apollo 11, the first manned mission to land on the surface of the moon. The culmination of my career was realized that day I took that momentous step and became one of the 1st of 2 men to walk on the moon.

There are many valuable life lessons I learned at West Point. The Cadet Honor Code, "A Cadet will not lie, cheat, steal or tolerate those who do," has influenced my life since Reception Day. I witnessed the timeless relevance of upholding the Cadet Honor Code and the impact of not, later in my career. During my Yearling year, a classmate was caught cheating and found guilty. He was up for Court Marshall, but the Commandant decided that there was not enough evidence and did not allow silencing. This cadet was later to become an academic coach for the football team. How that earlier Honor Code violation unfolded came back to haunt us with the infamous football cheating scandal of 1951.

Knowing what I now know, I wouldn't trade my experience at West Point for anything. Since graduating 55 years ago, much has changed at West Point, but the core values and mission remain the same - to produce leaders of character that will meet the challenges our nation faces in this ever-changing world.

BUZZ ALDRIN, one of the first of two men to walk on the moon, graduated from West Point, became a Colonel in the Air Force and flew fighter jets in the Korean War. He has a Sc.D. in Astronautics from MIT and was given the distinguished Presidential Medal of Freedom amongst many other awards. He founded Sharespace Foundation, a nonprofit organization inviting people of all ages to discover to discover the awe of space and fostering space exploration opportunities for everyone.

The **BEAR MOUTAIN BRIDGE** is only a short way south on route 9W from West Point. The view above is from the west side of the Hudson River. The area to the left in the picture is Fort Montgomery, part of the defense of West Point. If you follow route 9W south, you will come to the Bear Mountain State Park.

SURROUNDING AREA

West Point is located a mere 50 miles from New York City-one of the largest cities in the world. Yet in going the 50 miles from New York City, the urban atmosphere all but fades away and the mountains, trees and river take over. The area around West Point can only be described as rural. In fact the roads leading to West Point either from the north and Newburg or from the south and Bear Mountain Bridge, are still small two-lane roads winding through the mountains and clinging to the cliffs overlooking the Hudson River. This area would be worth visiting assuming that West Point was not there. But it should be noted that West Point is not easy to find and the roads can be difficult to navigate. In creating this book we often remarked that the British didn't try and take West Point because they could not find it. The only reason George Washington found it is he was a surveyor before he was in the military. Yet even today in the dark, in the rain or snow, it can be just hard to find your way to West Point. Take a map and check your directions carefully before you try and get there on your own.

West Point is located in Orange County in the Palisades Region of New York State. The Palisades actually encompass an area which stretches north from New York City about 150 miles along the west side of the Hudson River. In this region you will find amazing historical and recreational sites. After you have finished touring West Point, visit Fort Montgomery just north of the Bear Mountain Bridge. Fort Montgomery was part of the West Point line of defenses and is open to the public. Further north is the New Windsor Cantonment where George Washington issued cease fire orders ending the 8-year War of Independence in April 19, 1783. The site has staff in period dress and demonstrations at certain times of the year. Not far from there is the first state-owned National Historic Landmark, Washington's Headquarters in Newburgh. The site is along the Hudson River and depicts what life was like in General Washington headquarters. And if that is not enough of historic sites, there is Major General Henry Knox's headquarters at John Ellison's home in Vails Gate. General Knox was the Commander of the American artillery in the Revolutionary War. Besides these historic sites, there is Harriman State Park with 600 acres and 300 miles of trails and recreational facilities. There is also Bear Mountain State Park with a Wildlife Center at the Bear Mountain Inn. Bear Mountain State Park has great views of the Hudson River as well as a full range of recreational activities that could keep you busy year-round. This region also has the oldest winery in America, The Brotherhood Winery in Washingtonville. These are just a few of the things to do in the Palisades Region surrounding West Point

Just north and west of the Palisades Region is the Catskill Region which boasts one of the largest and most complex natural areas in the East. The Catskill Park is a 600,000 acre park and has been compared with Yellowstone National Park in its natural beauty. It has facilities for hunting, fishing and boating, horseback riding and snowmobiling. This is a year-round recreational facility that will keep you busy discovering new areas for years.

The area on the east side of the Hudson River is known as the Taconic Region and is equally rich in historical and recreational sites. This area is particularly known for it's stately mansions, scenic vistas and recreational facilities. Of note is the Franklin D. Roosevelt House which is open to the public. Not far from the Franklin D. Roosevelt House is the Eleanor Roosevelt House, also open to the public. Just across the way from West Point along route 9D is the little town of Garrison which offers great vistas of the Academy. Garrison also has some nice parks, restaurants and boat docks. A short way up from Garrison is the town of Cold Spring which has some equally good views of the Hudson River, some great bed and breakfasts and equally fine restaurants.

Highland Falls is West Point's immediate neighbor. It is a very small town with some incredible vistas of the Hudson River. It is a town where you will want to walk the streets and take in its small-town atmosphere. There are some good restaurants here but don't wait until after 9:00 p.m. to eat because everything closes down early. The West Point Visitors' Center is located in Highland Falls as is the West Point Museum. These are both starting points for your visit to West Point. Once you have finished your tour of West Point, remember the surrounding areas have a lot to offer.

ROUTE 293- BY FORT BUCKNER

ROUTE 293- BY FORT BUCKNER

ROUTE 293- BY FORT BUCKNER

PARK IN NEWBURGH

The photographs above highlight some of the scenic beauty of the **PALISADES REGION** on the west side of the Hudson River. Route 293 is miles of forested area which includes the Camp Buckner area of West Point. Newburgh is the town north of West Point on route 9W.

ROUTE 9W- ALONG THE HUDSON RIVER

ROUTE 9W-ALONG HUDSON RIVER

WASHINGTON'S HEADQUARTERS IN NEWBURGH

FORT MONTGOMEERY

Route 9W winds it way along the rocky cliffs of **HUDSON RIVER VALLEY**. The road has some breathtaking vistas, especially in the fall. Fort Montgomery, just north of the Bear Mountain Bridge is one of the original forts defending West Point during the Revolutionary War. Washington's Headquarters is another historic site located in Newburgh north of West Point.

153

HIGHLAND FALLS FROM THE VISITORS CENTER

HOUSE IN HIGHLAND FALLS

HIGHLAND FALLS - MAIN STREET

CHURCH IN HIGHLAND FALLS

The town of **HIGHLAND FALLS** is truly a small town and is the most immediate neighbor of West Point. At the end of Main Street is the Thayer Gate, the most known and used entrance to the Academy. Just before the gate is the West Point Visitors' Center and the West Point Museum. This is where most people begin their tour of West Point.

HIGHLAND FALLS is a quiet little town. It is a pleasant place to walk along the streets and take in the rural beauty of the area. There are some good restaurants here, but do not wait too late to eat because they "roll the streets up" after 9:00 p.m. in Highland Falls.

GARRISON- LOOKING OVER TO WEST POINT

THE TOWN OF GARRISON

GARRISON- LOOKING OVER TO WEST POINT

THE TOWN OF GARRISON

The **TOWN OF GARRISON** is right across the Hudson River from West Point. Here there are some really wonderful views of the campus from the parks along the river. Garrison is just a great little town to visit with its Victorian homes, quiet streets and boat docks. To get to Garrison from West Point go south on route 9W, go across the Bear Moutain Bridge and go north on route 9D a couple of miles.

CASTLE NEAR COLD SPRING

FARM NEAR COLD SPRING

ROUTE 9D LOOKING DOWN AT THE HUDSON RIVER

ROUTE 9D GOING TOWARDS CAMP SMITH

If you go south on route 9W go across the Bear Mountain Bridge, and proceed south on route 9D you will come to Camp Smith. The road to Camp Smith is an amazing road which winds along the Hudson River and offers stunning vistas. Going north on 9D a short drive past Garrison is another small town, Cold Spring. The scenery along the road offers beautiful landscapes pictured above, of castles on the hills, rustic farms and wet and wonderful views of the Hudson River. The area on the east side of the Hudson River is known as the **TACONIC REGION** of New York State.

157

MEGGITT DEFENSE SYSTEMS is proud to support the Army and the fine men and women of the United States Military Academy at West Point. Our weapon training systems range from virtual thru live with the addition of FATS products, which complement our air, sea and land targets and unmanned vehicles. You will find our ammunition handling onboard the Stryker MGS, Blackhawk, Apache, and future weapon systems. And our environmental control systems cool the Abrams, the electronics of the Kiowa, and next generation land platforms. Our systems go where warfighters go.

CORPORATE SPONSORS

The importance of corporate suppliers in meeting the Army's needs can not be understated. Suppliers are integral to the art of war and the importance in supply management is to have a supply strategy that meets the Army's requirements for success. The corporate sponsors in the following pages demonstrate that ability to foresee what will be needed and fulfill that need.

The commander in the field must know when and where logistical support will happen in order to succeed in battle, that the equipment supplied will offer troops the best possible protection, that the best radio and other technologies for communication and tracking the enemy are available and dependable, that transportation is both safe, reliable and fast, and that the best weaponry is available for soldiers to fight when necessary. There are many corporations that participate in the production of the end products used on the battlefield; some are manufacturers of the end-product and some manufacture critical components that go into the production of tanks, planes, weapons and some make or design the latest radar or IT technology, etc. The world is changing at a rapid pace making the military more reliant on modern technology and necessitating the use of private industry's innovations to maintain our technological superiority on the battlefield.

Sun Tzu is the author of the Art of War who is thought to have lived during the Wu Dynasty between the 6th century and the 3rd century BC. Sun Tzu's teachings form the basis of today's modern military thought and his work is thoroughly studied at West Point by cadets. He states that "Strategically speaking, to mobilise one hundred thousand troops you require at least one thousand chariots each drawn by four horses, one thousand heavy wagons fully loaded with ordnance together with one hundred thousand armoured soldiers and sufficient provisions to feed them as they march over one thousand miles. The cost of the campaign at the front and at home (including diplomatic missions and materials for maintenance and replacement of ordnance, chariots and armoury) will amount to approximately one thousand teals of gold in a single day." Few would argue with Sun Tzu that good suppliers and supply chain management are of vital importance to any army's ability to win. As Sun Tzu points out in the Art of War, it is impossible to accomplish any manufacturing and production without logistical support, never mind move an Army at war. Manufacturing, inventory, warehousing, packaging, handling of materials and transportation are all crucial to an Army's success as is a superior end-product. As technology becomes the dominant force of the new century, corporate suppliers who have top-notch engineers in touch with the latest technology and high-quality products, backed by an ability to produce at a pace in keeping with the needs of the Army as well as service products that have been sold, become more critical to our military in general.

Each company we have profiled in this chapter is participating in this book to demonstrate their support of the Army as well as their desire to provide our nation's army with the technology and products it needs to succeed in war. As you go through the pages that follow, please appreciate that these companies have what it takes to keep our Army on the road to victory.

STAFF MEMBERS DISCUSS SEVERAL BATTELLE PRODUCTS THAT SUPPORT THE ARMY MISSION

BATTELLE SUPPORTS THE D.O.D. WITH CRITICAL LABORATORY INFRASTRUCTURE

BATTELLE DESIGNED THIS MOBILE CHEMISTRY LABORATORY

WEST POINT GRADS: ELLIS '74, KUCHAR '77, BUCHA '72, ERTWINE '72, AND SUCHTING '75

BATTELLE is the world's largest independent research and development organization, with 20,000 employees in more than 120 locations worldwide, including five national laboratories Battelle manages or co-manages for the U.S. Department of Energy. Headquartered in Columbus, Ohio, Battelle conducts $3.8 billion in R&D annually through contract research, laboratory management, and technology commercialization. Battelle is a strategic partner to the Army, Department of Defense, and the Department of Homeland Security, providing science and technology leadership and innovative solutions to crucial national defense problems. As a non-profit organization, Battelle serves the Army as a trusted agent, providing an independent perspective backed by unequaled depth in critical fields of science and technology.

TEXTRON M1117 ARMORED SECURITY VEHICLE (ASV). One of the Academy graduates could end up commanding units which include the M1117 Armored Security Vehicle, produced by Textron Marine & Land, a Textron Systems company.   The U. S. Army has hundreds of fully armored ASV's in action today, with hundreds more being built.   These vehicles are able to withstand direct fire from .50 caliber machine guns and 12-pound anti-tank land mines under each wheel due to the 360 degrees of angled ballistic armor protection. The ASV can reach speeds in excess of 63 miles per hour, has flat-run tires, and has exceptional battle-proven firepower; all of which render this vehicle as mission-essential equipment.

The most reliable and highly tested semiautomatic pistol in history, the **BERETTA M9** has been the standard issue sidearm for the United States Armed Forces since 1985. After exceeding the grueling testing guidelines of the U.S. Military, the M9's accuracy, durability and ease of use has proven itself around the world—from Somalia to Afghanistan to Bosnia and Iraq. The M9's battle-tested performance and reliability have been continually enhanced during nearly two decades of service. In its seventh successful test, it improved from 17,500 to 21,000 rounds without a stoppage. The M9 is manufactured and tested at Beretta's Accokeek, Maryland plant, which employs 325 men and women.

RAYTHEON PATRIOT LAUNCHER

IMPROVED TARGET ACQUISITION SYSTEM (ITAS)

LONG RANGE ADVANCED SCOUT SURVEILLANCE SYSTEM (LRAS3)

RAYTHEON is a technology leader specializing in defense, homeland security and other government markets throughout the world. With a history of innovation spanning more than 80 years, Raytheon provides state-of-the-art electronics, mission systems integration and other capabilities in the areas of sensing; effects; and command, control, communications and intelligence systems, as well as a broad range of mission support services.

EADS NORTH AMERICA proudly salutes the U.S. Army, the Corps of Cadets and the "Long Gray Line."

Everyday America turns to its men and women in uniform to perform homeland security, medical evacuation, passenger/logistics transportation and drug interdiction missions as well as combat operations. And today the Army is looking to the **UH-72A LAKOTA LIGHT UTILITY HELICOPTER**, produced by **EADS NORTH AMERICA,** to aid its soldiers in fulfilling these vital missions now, and in the future. The UH-72A Lakota will allow older-generation helicopters to be retired and free up larger rotary-wing aircraft for assignment to other operational duties.

This cadet represents all that is the best of **WEST POINT** and the best to be. West Point is an incredible educational and military training institution which adds ethics and morality into the mix of what she molds. The end result is outstanding officers and leaders, and we thank West Point and our Corporate Sponsors for their assistance in making this book possible. We can only hope that it will begin to measure up to the high standards set by West Point and the Army.

DIRECTORY OF PARTICIPANTS

USMA Admissions Office
Building 606
West Point, NY 10996
Tel: 845-938-4041
admissions@usma.edu
http://admissions.usma.edu

USMA Association of Graduates
West Point, NY 10996
Tel: 800-BE A GRAD
www.aogusma.edu

USMA Bookstore
Thayer Hall 4th Floor
West Point, NY 10996
Tel: 845-938-5356
DSN: 688-5356
Fax: 845-446-1206
anita.schlier@usma.edu

U.S. Military Academy
Public Affairs Office
West Point, NY 10996
www.usma.edu

USMA Visitors' Center
West Point, NY 10996
Tel: 845-446-3085
8visit@usma.edu
www.goarmysports.com

New York State Department of Tourism
Tel: 800-CALL NYS
http://iloveny.state.ny.us

Battelle
505 King Avenue
Columbus, OH 43201-2693
Tel: 800-201-2011
www.battelle.org

Beretta
DoD Division
17601 Beretta Drive
Accokeek, MD 20607
Tel: 301-283-2191
Fax: 301-283-5111
aringerberg@berettausa.com
www.berettausa.com
(corporate) www.berettadefence.com

EADS North America
1616 North Fort Myer Drive
Suite 1600
Arlington, VA 22209
Tel: 703-236-3300
Fax : 703-236-3301
www.eadsnorthamerica.com

Meggitt Defense Systems
9801 Muirlands
Irvine, CA 92618-2521
Tel: 949 465 7700
Fax: 949 465 9560
dvolkland@wd.com
www.meggittdefense.com

Raytheon Company
Jim Etchechury
1100 Wilson Rd.
Arlington, VA 22209
Tel: 703-284-4484
Fax: 703-525-7738
jetchechury@raytheon.com
www.raytheon.com

Textron Marine & Land Systems
19401 Chef Menteur Hwy
New Orleans, LA 70129
Tel: 504-245-6600
Fax: 504-254-8000
Website: www.textronmarineandland.com